PRAIS

Having gone t[...]
dreaming of a[...] [...] Freedomunited.org (the world's largest antislavery community), I would highly recommend this book and the R7 process to anyone looking to go to the next level in their personal or professional lives.

—JOSEF SCHMIDT, FOUNDER OF FREEDOM UNITED

Dave really inspired me with this book, I was able to read it in 3 sittings, I loved the story of Kelly and Elliott, their faith-walk and how vision can win when you apply it to your life. Dave really captured my attention; I was totally locked into the story. A must read for coaches, athletes and all believers.

—RICK RANDAZZO, FOUNDER OF FCA HOCKEY

As a business owner that has gone through R7. I have seen firsthand how important Vision and how having a plan is essential for winning. It took me less than 4 hours to read this book, I couldn't put it down. I was inspired by the principles of R7 and goes to show how a simple process can make such a big impact in your personal life and business.

—RON KUHL, FOUNDER OF THE HOCKEY HUT

A heartwarming story with solid principles backed up with what's important in life.

—GLENN WESLEY, FORMER NHL AND 2006 STANLEY CUP WINNER WITH CAROLINA HURRICANES

As a former collegiate player, I was inspired by the book and how simple R7 can impact your life and give you direction for the next phase of sporting and personal career.

—JOSH HAMILTON
Liberty University College Hockey Player

Jesus was the master at telling stories and using them to teach us. In Vision Wins, Dave Jones is following in the master's footsteps, using an engaging story of two young athletes and their mentors to teach important lessons about life and faith. Set in "The State of Hockey," Minnesota, the story follows a boy and girl growing up hockey crazy achieving success in their highly competitive environment. Along the way they meet a wise Zamboni driver who mentors them about following higher purposes than even their athletic ambitions. Through another mentor they are introduced as teens to the Christian gospel and, through tragedy, learn to organize their lives and purpose around causes of lasting significance. The book gives practical insights into how Christians can define and pursue their purpose.

—BRIAN DENCH-BRYAN DENCH
Fellowship of Christian Athletes Hockey Board
Member, former high school and college goalie

This book was very inspirational to me, I really loved the mental toughness aspect for our athletes but also think it was an outstanding book for people looking for the next phase of their lives, everyone between the ages of 25-40 should read this book.

—KIRK HANDY
ATHLETIC DIRECTOR FOR LIBERTY UNIVERSITY CLUB SPORTS

I'm always looking for well-written business books that share how to better infuse my Christian principles into my day to day work. Vision Wins was just the read for that! As a hockey fan, I loved the story and while each character was special, I really loved the strength shown by Kelly in her support of Elliott. Be warned! You won't know what's coming as you follow Kelly and Elliott's R7 journey but prepare to be moved and motivated to bring to life your God-given vision."

—BAILEY ELDRIDGE, OPERATIONS MANAGER

My heart is full this morning. That's the only word that I know how to use to describe what I'm feeling…full of hope, full of excitement…very alive – today is kind of like its own little freedom adventure. I love it! I'm looking forward to more days with a heart full of purpose and destiny.

—DEBBIE VOSBURGH, BUSINESS OWNER

If you're doing what you love you're going to be better at everything that you do.

—ANNA FABER, Business Owner

Dave Jones helped me to get focused on the priorities and the things that are really important. It made me really understand why I had a passion in certain areas.

—DUPSEY OMOTOSHO, Pastor

I have more focus with all my passions - serving the community. I'm able to communicate what I'm here to do, and it's been great because I don't have to waste my time doing things that are not necessary for me.

—JACKIE OMOTOSHO, Pastor

You know the Reset Process for me, honestly, it just woke me up... It was an awakening.

—JEREMY WILLIS, CrossFit Athlete

It's a nice feeling when you wake up in the morning and know exactly what you want to do with your life. It gives you that kind of passion, that kind of energy, that I've been waiting for and I've been searching for.

—MYRON BETHEA, Global Vice-President

The biggest impact for me through this process was just having clarity and being able to have focus and priority and be much more productive in areas that really mattered.

—TROY HENRY, Audio Visual Recording Studio Owner

For me it means freedom... the freedom to be who I am all the time.

—RICK HOSTETLER, Ministry Leader

I have enough pieces now to move ahead, with confidence, without the fear, knowing that the possibilities are unlimited.

—BILL BARRET, Ministry Leader

It was really the key for me to find my peace in life. My life will never be the same. I have clarity and purpose now.

—VISH JETNARAYAN, Business Owner

What I got was the quickest, most powerful way of coming to the "why" in my life.

—BRIAN HISSONG, Ministry Leader

Once I hit [the Reset Button] it really gave me new life, and it gave me a sense of purpose.

—DAWN DURNIAK, Restaurant Owner

I found my vision. It reset where I wanted to go and how I want to be influential in the second part of my life. None of this would have been possible without Reset.

—GENE STRITE, Entrepreneur and Philanthropist

Becoming a Reset Specialist makes me optimistic about the future and gives specific direction on where to place my energy. It reassures me that I'm being proactive in my own life and that I'm taking control over the process to help others as well through teaching. Lastly, the process has allowed me to take my blinders off and be part of something bigger than myself, opening my eyes to be able to see more of the amazing world all around me.

—CURTIS WILLIAMS, Sales Manager

I grew up in a small town with little opportunity to allow me to pursue the things that I was truly passionate about. I was a dreamer. A high-level thinker. Difficult to stand still, I often like to fix things that aren't broken, and often re-invent the wheel. I love to meet new people, experience new things and help others see things they never saw in themselves. I love extreme sports and was blown away when I won a national wakeboarding championship at the age of 18. I started my first business at the age of 20. I got married to my best friend, Halee at the age of 22 and was able to travel around the world by the age of 24. My life was in the fast track and people often asked how I was able to get anything done. That was the problem... I couldn't. I was good at a lot but not great at much. I needed focus in my life and direction for the things I was strong at. Everything was going great but I needed to funnel my vision and have a plan for the rest of my life, not simply flying by the seat of my pants.

Then, Dave Jones of The r7 process entered my life. When I was introduced to Reset, it seemed as if it was designed specifically for me. I quickly learned what I was truly passionate about and how to develop a PLAN, which was a word I rarely used. This plan has been my guide and has been a pillar in building a very successful company, launching 3 offices and doubling our staff in less than 2 years. My Reset strategy has helped me pursue my dreams and goals as well as allowing me to pursue my biggest dream of helping others find their greatness. This is the very reason I jumped all in and became a Reset Specialist. Now I'm able to operate my business producing films and digital media as well as helping others pursue their passion. This funneling of my vision is why my personal vision statement is, "I Challenge Complacency". Yes it's simple, but it's me. It's powerful for my life and my vision for everywhere I go and everyone I meet. Life is good and Reset is helping me keep it that way!

—DREW JANES ,CEO
OF RELENTLESS ADVERTISING AGENCY

Sure, as a pastor I had a sense of why I was here on earth but going through the process to put it down on paper was exhilarating. Then, to finally read my own personal vision statement, lit a fire in my soul for me to, without apologies, go after the reason I was created by God to be alive right now. The Apostle Paul put it this way: I press on to take hold of that for which Christ Jesus took hold of me. (Philippians 3:12b NIV). Everything I do now is done with a new level of confidence because I know it is what I am supposed to be doing. I no longer wonder about what directions I should be taking. Every day is a day of clarity. It is all because I have a personal vision statement.

—ERNEST JONES, Senior Pastor

My time with Dave Jones clarified and crystallized my purpose and mission in life, allowing me to quit wasting time on "good" projects and instead spend my life in the "sweet spot" of my passion and purpose!

—RICK GREEN, America's Constitution Coach

Stu Epperson, President of the Truth Network, came to The r7 process to get his company back on track. Epperson describes his company before The r7 process as "scattered without a clear thought of what our mission and vision were. We didn't know where the company was going. The r7 process gave us a crisp, clear, and laminated statement of our purpose, our mission, and our vision. These guys helped us get our team together and helped everyone on our team know our DNA."

Personally thanks to Dave and his team for helping my company find out their specific goals, what God's plan is for the company, as well as exactly what himself and his coworkers are here on this earth to accomplish for the glory of God. Dave's team stepped up to help me and my company realize their true potential and vision. "I strongly recommend that you reach out to M is Good and let them come in and help your team, like they've helped ours.

—STU EPPERSON, President
Truth Broadcasting Corporation

The r7 experience was an adventure. I call it an adventure because I took a journey into my heart and soul to evaluate why I do what I do. Reset tools rekindled the flames in my heart that motivate me to be a designer in the present to build a better tomorrow. I appreciate the process and the reflection that continues today in my journey to transform negative mindsets, build constructive goals and connect people to build a better community. I am grateful for The r7 process.

—PAT TEAGUE, Former NFL Linebacker
for Cleveland Browns

The r7 process woke me up. Before I came to Dave and his team and I knew I loved one major thing: music. For many years I had toured around the country spreading God's Word through music at different churches, events, and musical concerts. I just knew that was what I was going to do. That is until my band broke up and I was left alone wondering what to do next. I was lost and didn't know where to turn. What I had thought would be my lifelong career in music was now at an end and I was alone. Just me and my guitar.

When I went through Reset, they really helped me realize that my two passions in life were obviously music but also the church. They helped me to really focus on those two key areas in my life and I started to put them together and lead worship at churches. I was then able to lock down a clear and concise vision statement for my life that is portable and to the point. With this vision statement, and the clear destiny path that I knew I needed to take, I found myself not only putting music and church together but landing a full time position in a church doing music. It couldn't have been any clearer for me. It's what I'm supposed to do with the rest of my life. I am grateful for The r7 process for helping me gain a clear vision and destiny for my life. I have Reset my life.

—COREY FOSTER, Pastor

Going through r7has made my daily life and decisions much easier. The r7 process uncovered things about me that I didn't even know about myself, but it was completely obvious after taking the steps through this program. It's all about you and discovering what makes you who you are. Going through Reset was better than any book I ever read or any conference or workshop I had ever been. It gets to the root and it's about you, not anyone else's experience. It's personal.

—HALEE JANES, Business Owner

The r7t process gave me a new excitement to life! I actually learned what made me tick, a full understanding of myself, and what my passions are. From there, I was able to move forward with the things that are important to me and say no to the ones that aren't important. I am excited as I achieve new things and know that there are many wonderful things waiting on me. Listen to the inner voice inside yourself and act on that voice!

—LAURA JONES, Founder of Hockey Mommy

My name is Subrina Berger. Every day, I capture moments worth sharing. What do you do?

The r7 process was shared with me by business associate, Drew Janes, during a time when I thought "eh, everything is ok, right now". But I attended anyway. After the general conference experience I was determined to get to Reset Island. (Yeah, it's everything you imagine it to be!) After my one-on-one Reset Experience I developed a Life Statement that really expresses who I am and who I want to be known as. The whole process in developing that single statement really opened up beneficial dialogue between me, Drew and Dave that left me feeling empowered, energized and fully capable of living up to my Life Statement, every day. I also had a plan. I had contacts to make that plan a success. I had something tangible to hold onto as I walked out the door. Someone other than me, had faith in me. Someone else believed I could attain the level of success that I envisioned for my future. I remember a testimony given during that first general conference that sparked a personal challenge in me. She said, "within days after my consult with Reset, I began to see miracles happen in my life". I wanted to know firsthand if miracles could happen for me. They did. And I am still feeling the effects of that miracle. My number one goal in this life is to be a mom, and Reset Agency put me in direct contact with others who could help make that happen...before I ever walked out the door of my one-on-one consultation. The r7 process is impressive, organized and all the things a motivational experience is supposed to be. But most of all - it's personal, honest and helpful. Three simple words that carry all the best answers to today's most burdensome questions.

—SUBRINA BERGER, Event Coordinator
and Ministry Leader

Dave Jones and the Reset Team were wonderful in helping me identify my core passions and developing a personal vision statement to assist me in the course of living out my true purpose. The plan that we developed together was specific with realistic and attainable goals to help guide me each step of the way. I would have never done this on my own and having their knowledge and support was key to moving forward with pursuing my destiny. My time spent with them was rich, meaningful and life-changing!

—DEBBIE VOSBURGH ,Ministry Leader and
Small Business Owner

The r7 process is incredible! I have already been talking about this experience with quite a few folks. I am very passionate about the radical potential this has in changing a generation and a culture. This is part of the plan of God to bring people into an understanding of "what they were created for". I am so sorry that for years I have been a part of the same machine that is so prevalent. That pumps folks like yourself to be all that you can and achieve your destiny but leaves you with no direction. I believe the scriptures would call that "clouds without rain". Thank God for Reset! Now, not only is it awesome to know our DNA so we can be a success, but we also have a responsibility to walk in this new knowledge. It has been amazing how many people agree with me when I quote my vision statement. It's like "yeah, duh" . If you have been honest through this process and have emptied out your soul, then your vision statement should not be a big surprise to those around you. Press on ! Resetting is the starting point, now go and become. The doors will open if you are being faithful to the true vision. A man's(or woman's) gift will make room for him(her).

—PATRICK BROWN, Model for Swiffer

If there's one thing I can't stand it's a bunch of touchy, feely, self-actualization bunk. Well, Dave and The r7 process are surely not that. Though they do help you uncover new and uncommon insights about yourself, it is done in a respectful, rigorous and systematic way. For me, it was a hard process and one that I needed some cheerleading to get through. Dave did just that when he needed to but he also called me on the mat just as often. More than anything, the r7 process helped me create clarity about where I'm going and what I want to accomplish in this gift of life. I'm forever grateful to Dave for taking me through a process I would have NEVER done on my own and becoming a friend who I know I can trust and lean on as I journey ahead. Thanks Dave for creating a process and place for me to "reset".

—JOE SCHMIDT , Former co-founder of
Canvas on Demand

VISION WINS

SEVEN STRATEGIES FOR MENTAL TOUGHNESS IN LIFE & SPORTS

DAVID A. JONES

R7 BOOKS
RALEIGH, NORTH CAROLINA

TABLE OF CONTENTS

FOREWORD

THE PRESSURE ON PLAYERS to perform at the highest level has created an identity crisis in our nation. It's true, we want to become the best version of ourselves, but at what cost? Seeking the acceptance of others, severe anxiety or stress? When we focus on accepting responsibility, having empathy, sacrificing for loved ones, family and friends, loving God, having trustworthy conversations, self-control, living generously, seeking God's approval not mans, encouraging other people around us and having hard conversations, we can begin the process of becoming a Godly person. There will always be trials and tribulations through an athlete's hockey career, whether it's in high school, juniors, college or professional hockey. At Northstar Christian Academy, we talk a lot about having a firm foundation, especially in the Gospel of Matthew. Ultimately, we want to amplify Godly traits in our life, when we have trials and tribulations we want a Biblical foundation, and this Biblical foundation is built on Jesus Christ.

Dave really inspired me with this book, I was able to read it in 3 sittings. I loved the story of Kelly and Elliott, their faith walk and how vision can win when we apply it to our lives. Dave really captured my attention. I was totally locked into the story. This book is a must read for coaches, athletes and all believers. Just like our culture here at Northstar Christian Academy, we are looking to build Godly world champions by communicating the Gospel of Jesus Christ one hockey player at a time. This book will certainly help any coach or athlete start their journey of becoming a world champion and warrior for the Kingdom of God.

Thanks Super Dave for inspiring us to become the best version of ourselves so that we can one day hear the words well done good and faithful servant.

—RICK RANDAZZO
FOUNDER FCA HOCKEY

DEDICATION

VOICES FROM THE FRONT

When I was first called to start Marketing Ministries, I was young and ambivalent, but excited to represent and help men and women of God with their vision. One of the great joys of these 19 years has been getting to know countless gifted men and women of God, practitioners of organizational learning managers, school principals, community organizers, police chiefs, business and Christian entrepreneurs, military leaders, teachers…people who have found an infinite array of imaginative ways to work with and utilize their God-given vision. In their own ways, each has created an alternative system of management based on the love of their Heavenly Father. I have so much respect for their willingness to serve God when they had no money and no time. They have fought through doubt, anxiety, and stress. I am humbled to be part of their journey in helping them with their vision, mission, and core values. If you are one of the over 400 organizations and ministries we have worked with in the past 19 years, I want to thank you for your trust, but more importantly, I want to thank you for being brave and intimate with your vision.

It's because of you, I have the courage to write this book. Working with men and women of God around the world has provided fresh insights into how master practitioners like yourselves have been courageous to initiate change and deal creatively with the challenges of sustaining momentum. In addition to many business successes, clients have revealed a host of new possibilities in applying organizational learning tools and principles in areas few of us could have imagined 19 years ago.

INTRODUCTION

OVER THE YEARS, I have realized there is nothing more powerful or captivating than a man or woman of God with a vision.

Purpose, passion and core values like perseverance, grit, hard work, accountability, and teamwork are all necessary for any vision to be carried out and communicated effectively.

We have learned that a project or organization will perish if there is no vision.

I have had many mentors over the past 20 years, from professional hockey players to c-suite executives and all of them had one thing in common. They all believed there was a better day ahead for them. They believed in a better tomorrow and didn't tear others down to get ahead in life. Even though hope is an extremely powerful concept and principle, they believed in more than the belief that change is possible, they believed in vision.

For me, it wasn't one meeting where the idea hit me like a lightning bolt, or that I had prophetic words or an audible voice from God. It was more of a grind; it was meeting after meeting. Three to five meetings a day brought me to the realization that vision is the North Star. Without that North Star, feelings of doubt, fear, anxiety, and stress begin to grow. Confusion and lack of communication upset the direction and execution of an executive team's agenda for the vision. Nobody is guiding the team forward.

A vision statement is a short, portable, easy to understand, memorable, and memorizable statement with no conjunctions or prepositional phrases. For example, you might say, I will:

- *achieve mind blowing dreams for a better world*
- *become the best teammate on the planet*
- *be obsessed with doing things better*
- *be passionate about living a life filled with divine purpose.*

Vision engages the amygdala. The amygdala is nested in the limbic system. This is important because emotions come out of the limbic system. The future you are fighting for is emotional and this is where vision is headquartered. Vision answers the "why change" question. The neo cortex answers the who, what, where, when and how questions. The neo cortex processes data. Processing data will not move humans to do extraordinary things. Data itself is important and powerful but it will not change a human being. Companies like Facebook and Instagram use data and information to manipulate the serotonin and dopamine in the brain. That manipulation can be positive or negative. If the manipulation is self-driven, it can leave a wave of devastation behind for family and friends to clean up. It can take a person in a discouraging direction. When vision is utilized well, it leaves the fruit of the spirit behind for the recipient of the vision, and family and friends.

When vision is effectively managed, everything else falls into place. The overall purpose-- the strategy, the brand, the communication, the prayer, and the action can each be executed. When these intangible items are executed, they provide one of the most powerful forces in the universe. When our vision is aligned with our Heavenly Father and we are executing His will for our life and we are glorifying Him with our passions, talents, and abilities, there is really nothing more powerful.

According to a Gallup poll from (2018), 68% of employees are disengaged at work. We are disengaged because we believed a lie. We bought into the idea that if we go to school, get good grades, and learn a skill, then we can someday get paid enough money for that skill and we will be fulfilled.

It doesn't take long to realize that sitting in a cubicle and constantly working for a superficial goal, like a new car or a bigger house, isn't actually satisfying our spirits. We want more. We are searching for deeper meaning and fulfillment.

Fulfillment comes through some level of self-actualization. Once self-actualization happens, we ignite our passion and purpose and begin to feel fulfilled.

VISION WINS

As Christians, self-actualization reflects God's amazing power, so that fulfillment happens. The Harvard Business Review and Gallup polls and News media research have all confirmed that people don't leave jobs or change careers because of money. Instead, what often motivates them to make a change is the need to feel valued, appreciated, and loved. They aspire toward a new vision to shape their lives.

Destiny awaits but time keeps marching on. We can reach out and shape our own destiny, by understanding our personal vision.

Our story here takes place in Minnesota's hockey world, but its message is for everyone. After all, we all want to have purpose and vision. Our inherent, God-given vision gives us clarity to move forward. Even if you don't have some form of a vision statement yet, don't despair, because it's there buried deep inside you, waiting to be uncovered and shared with the world!

The principles in this book are based on my life's work with Christian CEO's and athletes from all around the world. Its theories and applications will help you understand your personal identity, so you become the best version of yourself and help you lead small teams or larger organizations. Wherever you are in life, and no matter what work you do, your path will be only as strong as your vision.

Vision always wins!

(Super) Dave Jones
February 2021

CHAPTER ONE

DESTINY AND PURPOSE

Just a few minutes away from the hustle and bustle of Minneapolis is the quiet suburb of Edina, filled with big-city hockey dreams and home to some of the best athletes in the NHL (National Hockey League). Two teenagers in Edina with these NHL dreams were Kelly and Elliott.

Kelly and Elliott lived one block away from each other in a neighborhood in the city of Edina. Elliott lived on Brookview Avenue, and Kelly lived on Minnehaha Boulevard. The streets were separated by Minnehaha Creek and Arden Park. During the summer months, Arden Park was an area where local residents would take their dogs to fetch balls and kids would fly kites or play frisbee.

But from October to March, Arden Park was the place where NHL dreamers gathered together to play the sport they all loved. Local officials would flood the park with water, and Arden Park transformed into two glorious frozen outdoor ponds, now called hockey rinks. The park was so popular that local families had floodlights and a warming shack installed.

VISION WINS

The park, just minutes from both Kelly and Elliott's houses, was the epicenter for some of the most epic hockey games ever played. Almost every night someone from the neighborhood was at the park, imagining what it would be like to win the elite and incredible Stanley Cup.

Winning the Stanley Cup was every kid's dream. In their young minds they would visualize their families and friends watching them lift the Cup over their heads and skate around the rink. They could see themselves handing off the cup to their teammates and doing media interviews.

The kids from this neighborhood won the Stanley Cup a hundred times a day, and over the years it seemed like a million times by the time they were 12 years old. Every detail was rehearsed and played out in their heads. They could smell and taste their moment on the ice, with all the crowds and family members cheering them on to victory and celebration.

But before anyone could lift up the imaginary Stanley Cup, there had to be a game, with a hard-earned victory. The chirping or smack talk was just as epic as the game-winning goals. The pond had a heating shelter, and it was the best place to sit and warm up before and after games. Inside the warming shelter, all the kids would put on their skates, lace them up, and don their favorite NHL game jersey. It was a time-honored pre-game tradition. No one wanted to go home, ever!

DESTINY AND PURPOSE

For kids who loved to play hockey, the park was the best thing since the invention of the wheel, and Elliott and Kelly were no exceptions.

Kelly and Elliott were rarely on the same team and were pond hockey rivals. Elliott was two years older, but Kelly was a better skater. She could skate over and around him as if Elliott were standing still. Of course, nothing was ever organized. Kids just showed up to play hockey on the pond and it was game on. Hockey was everything to Kelly and Elliott. Some days after their hockey practice at the local rink, they would randomly meet to play at the park.

Elliott was one of the bigger kids in the neighborhood. He had a really hard shot, and most of his neighborhood buddies and local teammates were afraid of him. No one wanted to get hit with a puck in the shins or face. Most of his buddies wanted to be on his team because they wanted to win, and they didn't want to get hit in the head from one of his shots.

Elliott and Kelly each had dreams. At 12 years-old, Elliott decided he was destined to play for the Minnesota Wild and win the Stanley Cup at the Xcel center in Minneapolis Minnesota. Nothing in this world was going to change his mind. At 10-years old, Kelly's answer to "What do you want to be when you grow up?" was simple. She wanted to be the best NCAA division one recruit the world had ever seen and the first female NHL player.

They both imagined they would be pro athletes and spend every day playing the sport they loved. Their future dreams included making millions of dollars, buying amazing cars, and owning beach and lake homes. For each of them though, the most important thing was winning the Stanley Cup. Nothing else mattered; nothing could ever stop them.

THEIR PARENTS

Elliott's mom, Mary, worked at Best Buy as an executive assistant, and Steve, Elliott's Dad, was a Pilot for United Airlines. Elliott's parents were educated and worked hard. They were loyal to their families and friends and understood the value of money. They wanted something more for their children than they were able to have for themselves. They encouraged Elliott's dreams.

Like Elliott's parents, Kelly's parents, Karen and Dave, worked hard. They were well-educated and had great jobs. Dave owned two sports bars/restaurants in town, and Karen did the bookkeeping for the restaurants. They appreciated hard work, were successful business owners and were well respected in the Edina community.

Kelly's parents encouraged her professional hockey dreams because she was lightning fast on the ice. She didn't have a hard shot, but it didn't matter because she could skate. She would always be two to three strides ahead of everyone else.

Her older brothers thought she was annoying, so they were not nice to her. In fact, her motivation to skate fast was her way of proving she was tough and could compete. She always had something to prove on the ice and she proved it by scoring a lot of goals.

THE GAMES

Kelly and Elliott were across the creek pond hockey rivals. The Brookview avenue and Minnehaha boulevard kids were all about the same age and had some of the best pond hockey games. The games were one-goal games and there was always someone cheating. Sometimes they would make a no-goal call that was actually a goal, and other times someone was holding or running interference before or after a game-winning goal.

Series games were usually 3-on-3, and the first team to get five goals would win. If it was a best of seven series, you had to win by two goals. The games would take forever to play. In fact, it could take days, or even weeks, to complete the seven-game series. Kelly and Elliott couldn't wait to get home from school to either start or finish the series against the across the creek rivals. There were other rivals, but none compared to the Brookview and Minnehaha games. Most of the other games were blow-outs because the neighborhood kids from the other streets were either 3-4 years younger or older than each other. The kids from Minnehaha and Brookview were within six to eight months of each other, so their talents and abilities were about the same. They all played in the local youth hockey program together, but they were a gang of pond hockey brothers and sisters who loved to win at all costs. It was never a fair game when they played each other. The chirping and games were considered to be some of the most serious games ever played. It was all the kids ever wanted to talk about. It drove the parents crazy, but it was a real special group.

THE HORNETS

Everyone knew the Edina Hornets were winners. Only the best made it onto the team, and the pressure was always on.

Edina High School has produced over 200 state championship teams and hundreds of state champion athletes over the past forty years. The Hornets have noble graduates in the business, politics, entertainment, and sporting community from NFL to Olympic skiers, but most noble are the perennial NHL hockey legends from NHL General Managers to NHL Hall of Famers. The Hornets boy's hockey team competes in the top four hockey teams every year in the Minnesota High School Hockey tournament. The boy's teams have won a record breaking thirteen state championships and the girl's teams have won three championships over the past fifteen years. The business and sporting industries support the Edina community in both business and sports.

THE RELATIONSHIP

The spring of Kelly's freshman year, and Elliott's junior year, Edina got unusually hot in late March and it slowly became too hot to play on the pond. The ice was melting, turning back into slush and actual pond water. Before long, it would be impossible to skate on the pond in the park, and the pond rivalry would have to wait until Edina got cold again. So, the unfinished Minnehaha vs Brookview game turned into a street hockey game.

After three intense rounds of rock, paper, scissors, all the players agreed that the final game would be a home game for Minnehaha on Friday after school. The electricity and excitement of the game kept the whole neighborhood buzzing. Kids, parents, siblings, and friends were all waiting with anticipation for the final game.

One Thursday night, Kelly could not stop talking about what a jerk Elliott was and how bad Elliott's team cheated. Elliott had an alleged holding penalty against Kelly two days before and somehow the rest of the team agreed that it wasn't a penalty. Kelly would not let the holding penalty go. She was obsessed with beating Elliott's team.

Kelly's mother chuckled and said, "Sounds like he has a crush on you."

Kelly rolled her eyes and continued taping her stick in preparation for the big game, muttering about Elliott being a cheater, and how she was going to crush him in the game.

Later that night, Kelly's parents decided that one of them should be home for this epic game. Karen had placed a call to Elliott's parents to let them know she would take a sick day and supervise the game. Elliott's parents, Mary and Steve, thought it was fun and appreciated the call and were thankful Karen was able to stay home.

On Friday, once the kids got off the bus, they raced over to Kelly's house, arriving within minutes of each other. Karen had snacks prepared and water coolers in the driveway. The kids grabbed the street hockey nets out of the garage, yanked on their skates, and it was game on!

They were all excited, and wanted to start the game immediately, so the kids didn't even change from their school clothes. It was a sight to see.

Each player had Napoleon Dynamite Deluxe Custom moon boots, a green hockey helmet, green gloves, and a stick. There was a lot of slush on the road, and the ball didn't roll well, but the game felt like it was being played inside the Xcel Energy Center, with the neighborhood kids gathering around and cheering them on.

Kelly and the Minnehaha pond hockey team ended up winning that day. Elliott was just not himself. Kelly was not really fast playing in Napoleon Dyna-mite Deluxe Custom moon boots. Elliott could pro-tect the puck and shoot hard, so scoring was not a problem, but he just wasn't motivated to score.

DESTINY AND PURPOSE

Something else had happened that day that would forever change his view of Kelly.

When he arrived at Kelly's home, Elliott had to use the restroom before the game so he politely asked Kelly's mom, Karen, if that would be ok. She said the bathroom is down the hall to the left, past Kelly's room. Elliott responded with a hurried "Thank you."

As Elliott was walking past Kelly's room, the door was open, and out of curiosity he glanced inside, and what he saw in the room forever changed his perspective of Kelly. Kelly's room was neat and decorated. It was clean and glamorous, a completely different perspective to his NHL and ACDC postered room. On her dresser was a picture of Kelly and her family. It looked like they were on some tropical beach and everyone wore white clothes. Kelly looked stunning; she was absolutely gorgeous. Elliott was shocked that she had beautiful blonde hair and a nice body.

He was kind of bewildered, almost knocked off balance. In fact, he was emotional and mentally confused, almost dizzy. After about 45 seconds, he turned and walked down the hallway to use the restroom. He was confused because he had seen Kelly in school and at hockey almost his whole life, or at least as long as he could remember. For whatever reason, he never saw her through the lens of being a girl or a young woman. He only saw her as a competitor and rival. Today, he saw her as an amazingly beautiful woman. He reflected on how he always saw Kelly in a green hockey helmet, with green gloves on, and a stick in her hand. He had never seen her in a dress!

When he walked out of the restroom, before leaving, he made sure he cleaned up. He never really cleaned up his room or bathroom at home, but today, he paid extra attention to making sure he didn't leave a mess. It was as if he wanted to leave a good impression on his future wife's parents, and Kelly.

As Elliott was leaving the bathroom, he glanced down to the other end of the hallway and saw a large picture on the wall of Kelly in that same dress with the same tropical background. Elliott lost his mind. He was so amazed at how beautiful Kelly looked. She was hot and he couldn't get his mind off the transformation from pond hockey player in green helmet and green gloves, to how amazingly beautiful she was. Unable to resist, he walked down the hallway to get a closer look at the picture. He was bewildered and stood there for a few minutes just in awe.

Finally, he heard Kelly's mom say, "the game was about to begin." Elliott walked with a fast pace down the hall, somewhat dizzy, but trying to look normal. He walked down the hall and ran out the front door.

On his way out, Kelly's mom shouted, "Good luck" to him, but he didn't really hear what she said. Elliott was still stuck in his trance.

After seeing Kelly's picture with her feet in the sand

and in her beautiful white dress, Elliott knew he didn't want to play her or even beat her in a game of street/pond hockey. He had feelings and emotions he had never experienced before. Still bewildered, his heart raced as he tried to hide his emotions. He was awkward, not communicative, and not thinking about hockey.

Kelly and her Minnehaha Boulevard pond hockey team easily won that day and Elliott didn't care. He had fallen head over heels in love.

CHAPTER TWO

THAT SUMMER

From that moment on Elliott never played another game against Kelly. Instead of competing against her, he actively pursued her as a girlfriend. At first, Kelly brushed him off. The Minnehaha rivalry had run too deep, and there was no way she liked him. She was convinced it was a prank, or a way to throw her off her game.

However, after several weeks of honest talks, spending time together, and no longer competing against each other on the ice, Kelly realized he was serious. They went on their first date at the Convention Grill. It was a longtime neighborhood grill that had witnessed many late-night dates and proposals over the years; a local dive no one could resist. It was there that their friendship and relationship developed in a new way, becoming stronger day after day, and month after month. They became inseparable. Since this was Elliott's first attempt to date a girl and Kelly's first relationship, it was a new experience for each of them.

At first, Elliott's hockey buddies didn't understand. Elliott had two buddies who came over to his house on Monday, Wednesday, and Friday during the summer months after hockey was over and they worked out for 2-3 hours. Elliott had a sweet setup in his garage. His dad had built a rig in the back yard that had Olympic lifting weights, bars, barbells, kettlebells, sleds, and wall balls for the kids to use. He even had killer speakers in the garage where they could play any kind of music they wanted. His two weight-lifting hockey buddies were fire breathers; they were super fit and super strong, but more importantly, they were super fun. They would work out hard, but they loved each other's company. Joseph made everyone laugh and always lightened the mood when it was tense, and Timothy was just an amazing mule because he could keep moving with weight on his back for long distances. He was strong and had an engine like no other player on his team. He didn't have lots of talent on the ice, but he could out work and out lift anyone on the team. If you were playing against Timothy, you would not want to go into the corners to get the puck against him. He was short, but he could skate through anyone at any time and wreck you, much like a bowling ball taking down pins.

When it came to scheduling their lifting sessions, Elliott would have to tell his garage lifting buddies he was going to be late. Every other week during the summer he would text them at the last minute to let them know he would not be coming. Elliott was in love and was trying to spend as much time with Kelly as possible.

THE HORNET'S NEST

Braemar Arena is the home of the Hornets. For young players growing up in the Edina community, the high school hockey players were heroes, idols, and everything in between. Every home game was completely sold out. Hundreds of fans from all around the world come to watch the future NHL stars and Hall of Famers. It doesn't happen often, but when a 15-year-old freshman makes the varsity hockey team, it's not only packed in, its standing room only.

Elliott and Kelly grew up at Braemar playing on the west, east, and south rinks. Every week and every weekend when they were not playing pond hockey, they were at Braemar running around the rink. JJ was the Zamboni driver. His given name was Jeremiah James but everyone in the community called him JJ. Elliott and Kelly loved JJ because he was a gentle spirit, who loved to talk to the kids. If JJ wasn't driving the Zamboni or cleaning a locker room, he was more than likely engaged in a conversation with someone about hockey.

JJ, THE ZAMBONI DRIVER

Kelly and Elliott could not remember when they first met JJ. He was always at the rink and he was always available to talk. Today, JJ and Elliott happen to be standing at the Zamboni door together as they watch the Mini Mites finish up their practice. These young four and five-year old hockey players were all over the ice, tripping and falling on each other.

It was fun and entertaining to watch, Elliott and JJ would reflect back on when they first started to get on the ice. It was therapeutic to see since they had once been exactly the same way.

The high school team practices after the Mini Mites every Tuesday night at 7:00 PM. Elliott discovered how smart JJ was when JJ made a passing comment to him, back when Elliott was just a freshman in high school.

JJ said, "Elliott, someone once said to me, if you don't have a plan to win, then you plan to lose," and he just walked away.

Elliott immediately stopped him and said, "What does it mean if you don't have a plan to win, then you plan to lose? I have a plan. I am going to play in the NHL. That's my plan."

Elliott had a plan: to win a state championship with the Hornets, play juniors for one or two years and then maybe play one or two years in the NCAA Division I with the Golden Gophers. Then he would go right into the NHL. Since he made the high school team as a freshman, teams had already been calling him and his parents. He knew the NHL draft was in his future.

Elliott couldn't remember a time before that when JJ had said something of value to him, but he always liked JJ. Elliott was intrigued. Everyone liked JJ. In fact if you didn't like JJ there was something wrong with you. JJ was always talking with some-one and always had great stories.

After practice, as Elliott got undressed in the lock-er room, he paused for a minute to reflect on JJ's passing comment and he started to think about his relationship with JJ. The words echoed in his mind: "Someone once said to me, if you don't have a plan to win, then you plan to lose." Elliott couldn't get his mind wrapped around the message, so he began to think about his relationship with JJ.

He realized that JJ never really shared his personal life with anyone. Elliott couldn't recall a time where he was at the rink but didn't see JJ. JJ was always at the rink, behind the scenes talking with players, coaches, or parents. JJ loved to talk, but it was al-ways in the shadows of the rink, or when he was cleaning the ice. Elliott thought to himself, "JJ is always at the rink." Elliott began to get undressed. He needed to take a shower and get home. He had lots of homework and wanted to get to bed early. He had to pick up Kelly in the morning to take her to school.

As he was leaving, Elliott had one more thought about JJ. He thought he was talking to himself, but he said out loud, "JJ is a rink rat." His teammate said, "Don't say that about JJ, everyone loves JJ. Come on, let's get showered and get out of here."

WHO IS JJ?

JJ had worked in a small Christian Ad agency for over 20 years. He had started out in a traditional marketing agency as a media buyer and liaison for Christian organizations. He had a heart to maintain integrity and accountability of media buys between NBC, ABC, CBS and FOX television networks and Christian organizations. Because he worked with so many high performers, he saw an opportunity to build a process that would help executives and athletes with their identity and vision. So, he wrote, copyrighted, and licensed a consulting process called Reset Seven, which he later branded R7. In time, the R7 process was utilized by organizational leaders from all over the world. JJ helped them communicate their purpose through a well-articulated vision, mission, core values, and brand promise. Because JJ worked with Christian organizations for 20 plus years, he quickly realized that their process of communicating and executing their plan was inefficient. He realized most of them started with Action and he thought they should end with Action. He knew prayer was important and so was strategy and communication. It took him several years to fine tune the process. In fact, he tested the process on hundreds of executives and former pro athletes for about two years before he got paid for his time. He knew inherently that human beings were put on this planet for a purpose and their chief purpose was to glorify the Lord with their talents and abilities. JJ knew purpose should be the number one priority, but didn't think the word was fun enough, so he changed it to Destiny. After many years of trial and error, R7 became the process he used to provide clarity and direction to those around him.

The R7 Steps are:

1. Destiny: Embrace your DNA as your purpose
2. Vision: A Clearly Written Image for your future
3. Strategy: Formulate a Plan to Win
4. Brand: Build your Brand through all touchpoints
5. Communicate: Communicate your vision thru all touchpoints
6. Pray: Pray about steps 1-5, every day.
7. Action: Always move forward and never stop

When JJ was in his prime, he flew all over the world, meeting with high performing individuals who struggled or needed direction with their identity and vision. JJ charged a nominal fee and had each of them go through R7. JJ was educated, loved the Lord, and was highly committed to working with anyone who wanted to become a better version of themselves, regardless of their socioeconomic status.

He didn't know why, but one day, God sat him down and took him out of the starting lineup. So, JJ moved to the best youth hockey city on the planet, took a low paying job as a Zamboni driver and stayed in the shadows. He didn't like not being a star player for God, but he submitted to God's will. JJ learned early on to pray every day to be in God's will, but not to try and bend it.

Over several months, JJ felt God open an opportunity for him to be a mentor to both Kelly and Elliott. Because he was experienced in leading people with vision and purpose, and felt God awakening his spirit to help Kelly and Elliott, he started to engage Kelly and Elliott with steps to his proven R7 process. He didn't want to be coy with them, but he didn't want to give them the process all in one sitting. When he worked with his clients, it took several sessions over 7-8 weeks for JJ to help them, giving them homework, along with an hourly meeting each week. The executives, and former pro athletes who worked with JJ loved the process. He was always fully present and focused.

Now that God was opening this opportunity to him, he was super excited to help Kelly and Elliott, but he didn't want to overwhelm them with too much too fast. JJ knew it would be a frustrating road for Kelly and Elliott, but he also knew in the end, they needed to have ownership. So JJ took his time in delivering his process to Kelly and Elliott. Somewhere deep down in his soul, the Holy Spirit was telling JJ this was a special opportunity. Kelly and Elliott were going to make an impact on the world in a positive and productive way.

PLAN TO WIN

One Sunday afternoon Elliott and Kelly decided to go to the rink together. They both had away games on Friday and Saturday and wanted to get their skates sharpened before their Monday afternoon practice.

THAT SUMMER

They were standing in the hallway and talking about their games that past weekend, their goals assists and big hits, while their skates were sharpened by the athletic trainer. They texted the trainer the night before and asked if he could sharpen their skates before Monday's practice. The trainer thought it was strange but decided to help Elliott and Kelly out. They had had a successful weekend since both the men's and women's teams had won their games. The trainer was gracious to come in on a Sunday afternoon. As they were waiting, they saw JJ down the hall through the Zamboni door, so they both decided to go and talk with him.

JJ was welcoming as Elliott and Kelly approached him. "How can I help you, young man and woman of God?" JJ asked.

Elliott replied, "I can't stop thinking about what you said to me a while back."

JJ nodded and said, "I always like to see you two together. You are a real match made in heaven; you are a power couple. So, how can I help you?"

Elliott replied, "Thanks! Remember when you said to me that someone once told you if you don't have a plan to win, then you plan to lose?" I have been really thinking about that and I just can't get my mind wrapped around it. Kelly and I have known you since we were kids. Since we both started skating here, you have seen hundreds of great hockey players come through here, players like Brian Burke, Anders

Lee, Paul Ranheim, Kieffer Bellows, Jamie Mcbain, and Steve Fogarty. I just can't get my mind around why you would say that to me?"

JJ replied, "Young man of God, I am not as old as you think. I have never seen Brian Burke play, but I think I understand your point. I have seen player after player come through here and go on to play in the NHL, have great careers, get paid a lot of money, have nice cars, and amazing families. Some move back here and raise their kids in this beautiful community and others move on, but most importantly they all have something in common that is hard to escape. They have amazing intuition. I have seen you play, and I believe you will become one of the better players to come out of Edina. You will further the narrative of this city as one of the top areas to play in the world. I have watched you and Kelly grow up in this rink, and you both play a special game. I can see that you will also play a bigger role than you might think, because there is a bigger plan for your life. When you get a little older, before you leave here as a senior, I will share that bigger plan with you, but for now, I want you to know God loves you and has put you here for a reason."

JJ looked over Elliott's and Kelly's shoulders, gazing down the hall and said, "Looks like your skates are ready so, go on now. Get out of here and enjoy your Sunday. Get some rest, you have a big week ahead of you".

Kelly turned back and said, "JJ, why can't you tell

us now?"

But JJ was already walking away, so Elliott said to Kelly, "Come on, let's go."

As JJ told them to have a good night and enjoy their Sunday, he turned his back to them and started to head towards the Zamboni doors, the rest of the players were leaving the building, so it was time for JJ to drive the Zamboni and clean the ice.

Kelly and Elliott picked up their sharpened skates and left the rink. Each of them holding both of their skates in one hand, leaving their other hand free so they could hold hands with each other. They were a picture, something you might see on a hockey magazine cover.

INTERACTING WITH JJ

For the next couple of weeks, Elliott and Kelly were busy and they missed seeing JJ. One Thursday night, before her after school practice, Kelly crossed paths with JJ in the lobby of the rink. Kelly had arrived early to get about thirty minutes of stretching in before practice. She had finished her homework in the study hall at school. As she was walking into the rink, her eyes fixed on her iPhone, she didn't pay attention to what was happening. JJ was crossing paths with her. JJ was headed to the janitorial office to pick up some toilet paper and hand sanitizer for the family restrooms. He had noticed the supplies were low and thought he would put some extra rolls and bottles in the restroom, since there were four home games this weekend. Men's and Women's Varsity were playing at home against Blake, their section rivals. Last year they lost to them in the semifinals. The Hornets wanted revenge.

As Kelly was adjusting her iPhone, she looked up, and JJ said, "Hello, are you mentally prepared for this weekend's games?"

Kelly said, "I'm sorry JJ, I didn't hear your question. I saw your lips move but I couldn't hear what you were saying." She fumbled to find her volume control.

"All I heard was, are you mental?" They both laughed and JJ repeated, "Are you mentally prepared for this weekend's games?"

"The game is not until Thursday," Kelly replied.

He was just as taken back by her response, as she was by the question.

JJ said, "Mental preparation is a skill you have to practice, just like skating, stickhandling, or shooting. Do you only work on your stickhandling a few minutes before the game or do you work on it all week, like on Wednesday or Thursday before a weekend game?"

Kelly was on her heels. She was overwhelmed because it was a great question. She answered immediately, almost interrupting him and said, "I know the answer is I need to work on it during the week, but I have never practiced mental preparation. I have heard coaches say that I need to come to the rink mentally prepared, but I don't really know how to practice it; I don't know what I am practicing, or how long, or even when I should be practicing."

JJ said, "Walk with me."

As they were walking towards the janitor's room, JJ went in to get some supplies. It was a small closet so they couldn't both go in. Kelly reached for her phone and swiped up and swiped down and rushed to find her voice recording app. She had downloaded this app when she was in school. She loved studying human behavior and wanted to become a sports psychologist someday. She couldn't take official psychology classes until she went to college, so the best courses that overlapped with psychology were her social studies, biology and chemistry classes. She didn't want to miss anything, so she asked for permission to record the teachers during class. She liked to go back and listen so she wouldn't miss anything important. Kelly found the app and started recording just seconds before JJ came out of the janitorial closet.

JJ walked out with several bottles of hand sanitizer and rolls of toilet paper which he placed on the top shelf of his cart. The cart was old and squeaky and had a wobbly wheel.

JJ didn't waste any time. He said, "Your vision will always win, but we need to look at what future you are fighting for?"

Kelly thought this was a pretty simple question, but she didn't know how to answer it, so she said the first thing on her mind. In fact, as she was saying it, she thought.... *this is not my original thought.* She said, "My whole life, I wanted to be the best female hockey player in the state."

Kelly was sure that was the right answer. It came out smooth and it was something her dad, family, and local news would say about her. In fact, just last week she was the female athlete of the week in the state of Minnesota. The High School Hockey Coaches Association announced on Twitter that Kelly Martin was the athlete of the week, scoring two goals and three assists in last week's game, putting her in the top ten of the highest scoring female high school athletes of all time. As a Sophomore, she was sure to break into the top five before she graduated from Edina High School. So, her answer to become the best female hockey player in the state felt like the right answer. Kelly loved the answer, but she was still puzzled about the question. She quietly repeated it so the recorder would pick it up again as she wondered to herself, "What is the future I am fighting for?"

JJ and Kelly turned the corner of the mezzanine, where the restrooms were three feet away. JJ said, "I don't want to mess up your time here, since you are on the ice in twenty-five minutes. I need to drop off these supplies, so come by tomorrow or at the same time next week and we can talk more about your mental preparation and your goal to become the best female hockey player."

Kelly said. "I didn't really come to the rink early for mental preparation or to think about my future, I was coming to stretch, but I like the question and want to learn more. In fact, Elliott and I were talking about what you said to us a couple of weeks ago about our plan. Can we talk a couple more minutes? JJ said, "Sure, I can drop off these supplies after you leave to get dressed for hockey practice. Let's sit down. As they were sitting down in the stands, Kelly indiscreetly looked at her phone to make sure her phone was still recording. It was, and she was relieved.

They sat down and JJ said, "I think you and Elliott are very special to our Edina community and you will someday have a platform to influence many people. I see that you both have crazy talent and abilities."

Kelly interrupted him and said, "Yeah, we want to go to college together."

JJ didn't acknowledge her comment and jumped right into her vision to become the best female athlete. He told her she may or may not become the best female athlete in Minnesota. Then he went on to say, "Honestly, I am praying for you and Elliott to see a bigger picture than scoring goals and winning championships. Those are incredible goals and amazing achievements, but they should be your mission, not your vision. For example, your vision is like the peak of the roof, but your mission are the beams that support the roof. Another way to look at it is to say that your vision is your North Star, and it should answer the "why" in your life. Your mission statements are the steps to the vision and will answer the who, what, where, when and how questions in your life. True fulfillment comes from giving credit to God, your higher authority. You were created for something greater than yourself and when you recognize God's plan you will see that He wants to use you for something much bigger than scoring goals, and winning championships, or buying cars and making lots of money. Don't get me wrong, these are all great achievements, amazing accomplishments, but someone wise once asked me if I ever saw a U-Haul behind a hearse.

Kelly was a sophomore in high school, and she had a 3.8 GPA. She was very smart and articulate for her age. Even so, she didn't understand a word JJ was saying. She was so confused. Her whole life up to now, had brought attention and accolades because she could skate fast and score goals and was a great hockey player. Her identity of being a hockey player was molded into her DNA. What was a bigger picture? What did God have to do with it? These were all new ideas that she needed to ponder. She looked at her phone, and the audio was still recording, but she had to be on the ice in seven minutes!

She said to JJ, "I am sorry, but I need to get on the ice for practice. Coach is going to kill me if I am late. Can we talk later?"

JJ said, "You know where to find me."

Kelly got up and dashed down the stairs, hopped the guardrail, disappeared into the tunnel, and ran to her locker room. Six and half minutes later she was running onto the ice, snapping her helmet shut, and skating to the huddle at center ice, as she put on her green gloves and got situated. As she took a knee and listened to the coach give out instructions for the first drill, she glanced up at the seats where JJ and she had been sitting. She saw JJ come out of the bathroom, no longer bearing supplies on his cart, and disappear around the corner of the mezzanine.

Later that evening, as Kelly was getting ready for bed, she decided to listen to their conversation before she went to sleep. As she was listening, she got out her journal and wrote

Vision: What is the future I am fighting for? (Mission: hockey player)

CHAPTER THREE

PREPARING FOR THE GAME

This was Elliott's senior year. He didn't have many home games left, so he wanted to cherish every moment. He arrived especially early for the game. He would normally arrive ninety minutes before game time, but tonight was a big night against their division rivals so he was there three hours before puck drop. He sat halfway up on the home side stands where he was able to look at both benches. He visualized himself jumping off the bench, taking three hard quick strides, jumping into a passing lane and driving wide across the blue line. He could see himself in the perfect position to make a pass to his trailing line mate or beat the defender. He noticed the defender was left-handed and his stick was in the air, so he had an extra half stride on him. He was visualizing going to the net or making the pass. He really wanted to go to the net because he loved to create chaos in the crease and allow his teammate to bang in an easy goal. Yes, he could see himself sacrificing his body by driving to the net. The moment he thought about going to the net, he remembered JJ's words "Are you mentally prepared for the game tonight?"

Elliott was totally into visualizing this play. He could see it, feel it, and taste the sweat coming off his nose and into his mouth. He could hear the crowd and the sound of his edges gripping the ice. He was so into it; he could even smell the popcorn shared by the crowd. In his mind, he heard JJ's voice again: "Are you mentally prepared for the game tonight?" Elliott looked up just as JJ sat down.

"Oh, hey JJ, "Elliott said. "I am here visualizing the game. I love to put myself into the game. It helps me prepare and focus. Elliott changed the subject and started to say, "Kelly had me…" and he paused, because at that moment he was going to say, Kelly had me listen to your conversation the other day. He caught himself before he continued, because He forgot Kelly told him not to say anything about the recording.

"Ah sorry," he said, "I was thinking about the game." Elliott straightened up and shifted himself in his seat and said, "Kelly said you asked her what future she was fighting for."

JJ said, "Yes. it's important to have a future vision. It's something you will want to work out for yourself." JJ changed the subject quickly. It was not that he was put off, but he didn't think it was the right time to talk about future vision before the game. He knew Elliott was here to mentally prepare for the game and the topic of vision was a much larger question to work out.

JJ said, "Elliott, I have seen a lot of games in this

barn and one of my favorite ways to watch the game is by observing the emotions of the game. Do you ever not watch the x's and o's of the game, and watch the emotions of the game instead?" Elliott had never considered that before, and he replied that the only emotion he ever felt was frustration when he missed the net or when one of his teammates received a stupid penalty.

JJ went on, "Yeah that's how I understood emotions when I played. Later on, I learned there are as many as six warning signs that suggest you can be a slave to your emotions. It's a big topic though, so we can talk about them later when we have more time." It's interesting though because I also learned that there are actually over 272 core emotions. When we are a slave to our emotions, we are not in control. In a game like hockey, it means we can take stupid penalties or in the game of life, we can say something stupid to our loved ones. Interestingly, when you are a slave to your emotions you always have regret. For me, that's one reason I don't use social media anymore, because people usually post things out of pure emotion. I have lost friends over the years because I was a slave to my emotions. In hockey, one of the tricks to playing at the upper ranges of your ability, consistently under pressure and in the biggest moments of a game is to have the ability to be a master of your 272 core emotions. Have you ever wondered why some players take dumb penalties and other players don't?"

Elliott looked at JJ and said, "I guess I haven't stopped to think about it."

JJ replied, "Well, some players have empathy. Do you know what empathy is, Elliott?"

Elliott said, "I'm not sure I know what you are looking for."

JJ continued, "Empathy is about relating to others, but before you have empathy you have to be aware that you have low EI."

"What is low EI?" Elliott asked.
JJ explained, "Low EI is Low Emotional Intelligence. It is when you don't have awareness of your surroundings. You don't understand the feelings of others. You don't love yourself, your teammates, your coach, or your organization in ways that can make a difference."

Elliott asked JJ one more time, what empathy was. JJ looked him right in the eyes and said, "Empathy is when you see and understand other people's feelings. When you are aware of your own feelings, you also process other people's feelings, and you become the best version of yourself. When you are able to do this, you have High EI, or High Emotional Intelligence. When your teammates have Low Emotional Intelligence, they are emotionally draining to be around. They don't care about anything else but themselves. They don't care about others and often leave a wake of devastation behind them for others to clean up. They need constant hand holding and are difficult teammates and may even be difficult family members. Do you have any of these people in your life right now?"

Elliott thought for a second and said, "Yes, our back-up goalie this year is a guy named Adrian. I imagine he is Low EI since he doesn't seem to have any empathy or awareness. He's pretty caught up with himself. Yes, I can see that now." As Elliott pondered that, he realized Adrian was starting that night!

JJ went on to talk more about emotions and being a master to them. Elliott was respectful and listened, but his attention was divided. He was half thinking about Adrian and half listening to JJ.

JJ went on to say "When you are a master of your emotions, you are not just a better hockey player, but you are a better human being. God created emotions for us to use wisely and well. They are a powerful force when they are used correctly and sometimes an even more powerful force when they are not used correctly. They are sort of like money. Money is amoral and so are emotions."

Elliott spoke up, "Wait, what's this about emotions and money? How are those two connected".

JJ explained how emotions and money are amoral. Money is good in the hands of good people, and bad in the hands of bad people. Money has no moral code of its own. It's amoral in the sense that money cannot determine if a situation is right or wrong. Emotions are the same way. Emotions can be good when a person is in control of them and understands the bigger picture. The bigger picture is God's plan, but it can also be the bigger picture of a player, hockey team or organization. Of course, emotions can be used by bad people who want to manipulate others into doing bad things.

Elliott responded, "Ok, so what I hear you saying is that some people are Low EI because they don't care about their team or don't care about themselves? These players are slaves to their emotions."

"Yes, that is correct Elliott," JJ said.

"Not to change the subject," Elliott said, "but what is your vision JJ?"

JJ quickly said with confidence, "My vision is to unify excellence in the marketplace."

They both looked out at the rink as if something were happening, but the rink was dark and quiet. They just sat in silence. If anyone was watching them, the scene would have appeared weird and awkward, but to JJ and Elliott there was a game going on and they were watching everyone's emotions ping back and forth. They were visualizing and experiencing a game of hockey with Low and High EI situations.

PREPARING FOR THE GAME

GAME TIME

> *O, say can you see by the dawn's early light*
> *What so proudly we hailed at the twilight's last gleaming?*
> *Whose broad stripes and bright stars thru the perilous fight,*
> *O'er the ramparts we watched were so gallantly streaming.*
> *And the rocket's red glare, the bombs bursting in air,*
> *Gave proof through the night that our flag was still there...*

As the last half of the National Anthem was playing, Elliott was going through his game prep plan. He instinctively knew he had to focus. He was not sure where he learned to do this, but during the National Anthem, he would become hyper focused on the environment. It didn't matter if they were home or away. He would park all his other thoughts, issues, or concerns he had with his family or school life. He instinctively knew that his issues and concerns were not less valuable or less important, but he had to focus and have the ability to refocus on the task at hand. He wasn't into rituals, but he liked to say he had routines or checklists he went through. For instance Elliott said underneath his breath, one stick in his hand, no helmet on, feet slightly moving back and forth, "What do I smell?" He smelled the awful smell of his shoulder pads, a smell that was mixed in with a clean game jersey. Then he whispered to himself, "Ok got it, what else do I smell?" He could get a whiff of the brisk air in the rink, not really a smell but he could feel the cold ice. He took a deep breath so he could feel the breath go into his lungs and his diaphragm and then he exhaled, making sure his exhale was longer than his inhale. He could feel his shoulders and then his entire body relax, and he knew he was officially focused.

He whispered to himself, "What do I hear?" He closed his eyes, and he was visualizing himself shooting the puck and the puck hitting the right side post, that sharp ping sound of the puck hitting the post, and then ricocheting off the goalies pad and going into the back of the net, and he could hear the school band and the crowd go crazy, He could see, hear, taste, smell and feel his teammates rush over to him, give him a hug, as they all skated over to the bench for a train of high fives. He was ready to play. He snapped out of his mental prep routine to hear a 10-year old local Edina girl finish singing the national anthem

> *O say does that star-spangled banner yet wave,*
> *O'er the land of the free and the home of the*
> *brave?*

PUCK DROP

The game was tied 1-1 and going into the third period. Puck possession was back and forth, the Edina Hornets and the Blake Bears had energy; both teams were moving the puck and getting quality shots on the net. The play was back and forth and up and down the rink, and the crowd was on the edge of their seats. It was a hard-hitting fast-paced game. The media talk leading up to the game was everything everyone was expecting to watch. Elliott worked hard throughout the game. His shifts were quick, and he was fast on his feet, pivoting heels up ice. He was always in position and dialed in, trusted, calm, relaxed, commanding, confident and smooth.

He made the game look simple and easy to play. He had several opportunities to score, but just wasn't finding the back of the net. He remembered his talk with JJ, when he was on the bench or when he was backchecking. He was thinking and saying to himself "Power Channel, High El." He didn't know where "Power Channel" came from, but he liked it. With seven minutes left in the game, he took the puck wide into the offensive zone, and passed it back to the trailing line mate. The trailing line mate passed it over to the other side of the ice to his right-handed wing playing on the left side. His line mate pulled up to create a lot of space and immediately passed the puck to Elliott who was streaking to the net, and who is a left-handed shot. Elliott times the shot perfectly; the puck hits the goal post and ricochets over to the other side of the post. It hits that post, a double ping sound echoes through everyone's ears, and the puck drops into the back of the net.

The crowd goes wild, the marching band goes crazy, hugs and high five train at the bench. The Hornets go up 2-1 with six and half minutes left in the game.

There was a turnover at center ice and a 50/50 battle ensued between the Blake defender and the Hornets right winger. The Blake defender won the battle, took three hard strides to get to the center ice line and shot a hard shot towards the corner of the ice. It seems to be a routine dump in, so Adrian goes around the net to stop the puck, making it easy for his defensemen to pick up the puck behind the boards and either skate it out or make a great pass to the forward. This was a routine play for most goalies to make and it was especially routine for Adrian. Adrian was tracking the puck in the air. He clearly understands the puck is going to hit the glass, go into the corner, pick up a little speed as it goes into the corner and come to the back of the net on the boards. He will stop the puck first with two hands on his stick and then gently pull it halfway between the back of the net and the boards. As Adrian goes behind the net to get the puck, the puck hits the glass and travels about thirteen inches, takes a weird, almost never seen before bounce off the boards, and is now traveling very fast directly towards the empty net.

Adrian reacts as best he can, but trips on his stick. He falls to one knee awkwardly and loses all of his momentum as the puck goes into the back of the net. The home crowd goes silent. The away crowd goes crazy and everyone looks back at the Blake defenseman who routinely dumped the puck into the zone. Players skate over to give him an awkward hug because he scored, and it is what you do when your teammate scores. But it was weird because he didn't mean to score. He scored because of a weird bounce, not because he ripped the puck past the goalie or had a crazy deceptive move. All five players skate towards the Blake bench for the high five train. The entire crowd looks at the referee, who signals a goal and skates to the scorer box to give the score and says, "Unassisted goal by number 38." Everyone looks at the score clock hanging at center ice. which goes from 2 to 1, to 2 to 2. Most everyone in the building was disorientated but accepted that it was a good goal.

No one blames Adrian that the puck took an awful bounce, and the people in the crowd who have been around hockey for a while have seen this before, but it's very rare. The people who are new to hockey were completely amazed by the goal and the turn in momentum. The home crowd is bewildered; the away crowd is excited.

1:49 LEFT TO PLAY

Inside, Adrian is frustrated, humiliated, and withdrawn. His emotions are running rapidly, and he is completely out of control. His heart is racing faster than it has ever raced in his entire life. For him, it wasn't so much about the goal, it was that he tripped trying to get to it. Of course, no one in the crowd could see his emotions, you couldn't see his face, and his body language was not drastic, but inside he was a mess. Adrian had never really experienced these emotions. All eyes were on center ice to see what was going to happen next, all eyes except JJ's eyes. JJ's attention was on Adrian. JJ had seen this before and he knew it was not going to end well.

Blake won the center ice faceoff and the winger immediately dumped the puck into the Edina offensive zone. It was a similar shot but didn't have the same speed as the earlier one. The Blake forwards had a new energy, and they were inspired by the change in momentum. The puck rims around the corner and goes behind the net. This time Adrian doesn't go behind the net but stays in his crease. The puck goes across to the other corner. Both the Hornets defenseman and the Blake forwards are racing for the puck and it looks like another 50/50 battle. As the Blake forward comes across the crease, Adrian takes his goalie stick to his hip level above his goalie pads but below his waist. He looks like a baseball player but has a goalie stick in his hand. The stick was not at his shoulders, like a true baseball player. He raised it to his waist and swung his stick at the Blake forward like he was chopping down a tree or a batter at home plate. The Blake player slides across the ice and like a bad movie scene, the referee signals for a penalty. A second later, he calls a tripping penalty on Adrian. The home team sits in their seats in disbelief and JJ whispers to himself, "Here we go."

It took 32 seconds for Blake to score a goal. The Hornets were down 3-2 with 27 seconds left in the game. Elliott won the faceoff back to his defensemen. The defenseman took three hard quick strides and shot the puck into the Blake offensive zone. The Edina coach signaled for Adrian to come to the bench so they could put another attacking forward on the ice.

Adrian knew what the coach was doing, so he skated as hard as he could to the bench. When he got to the blue line, he tripped over his stick again, and went sliding into the bench. He tried to stop his momentum, but it happened too fast and he slammed head-first into the front of the bench. He quickly got up and slammed his stick against the top of the bench. The stick broke and flew up. As it flew up into the air, the assistant coach and about seven players sitting on the bench covered their eyes from the debris. The assistant coach ducked like he was dodging shrapnel from a grenade. As the shattered stick was flying in the air, the Blake player gained possession of the puck in his defensive zone and shot the puck all the way down to the other end of the rink some 200 feet away. The puck went into the empty net and the scoreboard read 4-2.

The shrapnel from the stick had landed on the players on the bench and the assistant coach and trainer. A moment later the puck was in the back of Edina net. Blake went up by two goals with only three seconds on the clock. Adrian didn't go back in the net for the remaining three seconds, but he left the rink embarrassed, bitter, and defeated. No one said anything to him; they just let him go. The starting goalie hustled to put on his helmet and gloves so they could drop the puck at center ice to officially run off the remaining three seconds and finish the game.

THE NEXT DAY AT PRACTICE

JJ and Elliott unexpectedly met at the Zamboni doors again the next day. JJ had been standing there first. Elliott walked up behind JJ, who didn't turn to say hello because he was just watching the Mini Mites play. They had about four minutes left in their ice time and JJ had to jump on the Zamboni to clean the ice for the Hornets varsity team. Elliott didn't say "hi" or "hello" as JJ was staring at the Mini Mites. Elliott waited for about thirty seconds and said, "Low El." JJ responded, "Low El." Elliott had about fifteen minutes before he had to get dressed and be on the ice for practice, so he turned and walked back through the tunnel to his locker room. He was not looking forward to seeing Adrian, or even being in the same room to hear about last night's game.

GOOGLE HANGOUT

After practice, Kelly and Elliott were talking about their weekend. Kelly's team had swept Blake both games and won by four goals each game. They dominated the weekend. In fact, it was an easy weekend for Kelly. Most of her teammates were not challenged either. They didn't talk much about Kelly's games because there really wasn't much to say. Elliott was anxious and excited to talk about his game with Kelly.

Elliott said, "This weekend was really interesting, I went to the rink early to do my mental game prep and JJ sat down with me. Kelly was listening and walking around the house, but as soon as Elliott mentioned JJ, she did a double take.

She said, "Wait what? You talked to JJ?" Kelly walked briskly to her room, scrambling to find her journal.

Elliott said, "Yeah, I had the most interesting conversation with JJ. He talked to me about being aware of my emotions, empathy, and watching the emotions of the game. At first, I thought he was crazy, but after yesterday's game, I think he is a genius, like for real."

Kelly said, "Tell me more," as she reached down to the bottom of her dresser and pulled out her journal. It was under her three pairs of black Gym Shark training leggings. "There it is," she whispered.

Elliott said, "There what is?"

Kelly replied, "I found my journal where I am putting all of my JJ notes."

Elliott said, "Ok, well as I was saying…. I think JJ is more than a rink rat. He was talking to me about High EI and Low EI."

"What is EI?" Kelly asked.

Elliott explained that EI stands for Emotional Intelligence. "An example of low EI might be if someone slashes you in the back of the leg and you thoughtlessly retaliate and slash back because you don't care about yourself or your team. JJ said when you do that, you are not in control of your emotions. He actually said that you are a slave to your emotions."

Kelly said, "Please, go on."

Elliott kept talking and said, "Yeah, so if someone slashes you in the back of the leg and you don't retaliate, that's called High EI. In this situation you are master to your emotions.

"At first, I was only sort of interested in what he was telling me. I was respectful and made a mental note of it, but now as I reflect back on our conversation, I think about Adrian tripping that player and when he couldn't get back to the net, they scored. And then a couple of minutes later, he chopped down the Blake player as he was skating through the crease. He chopped him down like he was cutting down a tree! I could see Adrian go Low EI, and remembered what JJ was telling me. I mean I could see the words over his head that read "Low EI" and the words were flashing over his head like a red neon sign… Low EI, Low EI… over and over again. I thought to myself, JJ was right. JJ had just talked to me about this and I was seeing it unfold right before my eyes. I was so blown away and then when Adrian tripped and hit his head on the boards, that was just disappointing and awful all in the same moment. Kelly, we need to talk to JJ about how to get out of that vicious cycle."

Kelly agreed and made some notes in her journal,

including, *Build Awareness of High and Low EI.*

THE MASTER PLAN: COLLEGE AND PRO HOCKEY

Elliott and Kelly loved each other and for the most part everyone in the school loved them. It had never been done before, but school officials allowed Kelly to be Elliott's queen his senior year. Everyone could see they were a power couple. Elliott and Kelly were outstanding hockey players; they both scored a lot of goals and were great teammates.

Elliott declined the verbal offer to the Golden Gophers and accepted an NCAA Division 1 offer to Saint Cloud State. He wanted to be a Golden Gopher, but the situation just didn't work out. The community was excited for him. Elliott was a good student but didn't really care about any particular field of study, so he figured he would be a business major.

Kelly on the other hand, was excited about becoming a sports psychologist so she loved the idea of going to Saint Cloud. It was close to home and she was sure she could play hockey for them as well. Elliott was going to play one or two years of Juniors, then Kelly and he would meet at Saint Cloud, play hockey for the same school, get married during Elliott's 1st or 2nd year of pro. Elliott and Kelly knew he was headed to the NHL. As an NHL player he could help pay off all of Kelly's college debt, live in Edina and raise a family while Elliott played in the NHL. They were pretty sure Kelly was going to get a scholarship to play there as well. She was one of the best female players in the state, so getting an offer was going to happen. Since she wanted to pursue a Doctorate in Sports Psychology, they knew they were going to need extra money to pay for her schooling. They had talked about this almost every night. How she could help him with his playing as a sports psychologist and he could support her schooling. Kelly and her parents looked at the cost of advanced college degrees that Kelly would need to pursue her masters or doctorate to be a certified sports psychologist or certified mental performance coach. Kelly and Elliott had their path figured out and there wasn't anyone in either of their families who had any push back. They were both great students, great teammates, and they both had elite talents and abilities. They were a power couple, they loved each other, and nothing was going to derail their master plans.

KELLY'S SOPHOMORE YEAR

Kelly's team won the state championship again in her sophomore year, which was the second time she had won it. She led the team in scoring and assists in the game and for the second straight time, she led the team in scoring all year. She might be the first girl to win four state championships.

ELLIOTT'S SENIOR YEAR

Elliott's team also won the state championship. This is also Elliott's second year to win it. Elliott won as a Freshmen and now as a Senior and as a captain on the team. Elliott also was the team's leading scorer. Elliott had more goals than assists. Immediately after the state championship, Elliott was invited to skate in the United States Hockey League (USHL) with the Fargo Force.

THAT SUMMER BEFORE JUNIORS

Kelly and Elliott thought it was the coolest thing to label the next summer, the "summer before juniors." Kelly was going to be a junior in high school and Elliott was going to play his first year in Juniors with the Fargo Force. Elliott was super excited to play for Fargo. The USHL has teams all over America and most of the teams are west of the Mississippi River. Elliott was extremely grateful to be less than four hours from home. He could have played for any USHL team, but to be playing in Fargo was a blessing.

One Thursday night after practice, Kelly and Elliott saw JJ and he asked Elliott if he would like to go to a "College and Pro Camp" and train for a week. Elliott had never been to a "College and Pro Camp," so he was instantly excited. Elliott emphatically said, "YES!"

JJ said, "Ok great! I will let my buddy Ranger know you will be coming."

As JJ was leaving, Kelly looked at Elliott and whispered, "What about me? I want to go. Can I ask JJ if I can go? Or is it a boy's only camp?"

Elliott shrugged his shoulders and didn't know what to say. Kelly said, "Hey JJ, what about me, can I go?"

He looked back at her and said, "Sorry, Kelly. I think the girls camp is the week after the College and Pro Camp. The College and Pro camp is for boys only. I will check into it. Have a great night."

Within forty-eight hours, Ranger, the founder of FCA Hockey, called Elliott to say how happy he was that Elliott would be attending the College and Pro Camp at NorthStar Christian Academy in Alexandria, Minnesota, which was just two hours northwest of Edina, and Kelly would be going to the girls camp a week later. Kelly and Elliott were excited about their new adventures. Both Kelly and Elliott had passed Alexandria many times in their youth hockey careers playing games in Fargo. Though they were familiar with the drive, they had never stopped in Alexandria to play, which now they thought was kind of strange.

Both Elliott and Kelly were excited about the camp, but they didn't know what to expect. Kelly never talked with Ranger Richard, but she trusted Elliott's conversation with him. Elliott admitted that his phone call with Ranger was overwhelming because he talked fast, but with confidence. Elliott trusted JJ, so he trusted Ranger. Elliott was not sure why JJ invited him to the camp since he wasn't in college or a pro. Ranger talked about the talent, but also the faith aspect of the camp. Elliott was more interested in the competition of the camp and he didn't really think about the faith aspect of it at all.

PREPARING FOR THE GAME

Elliott arrived at camp and everyone welcomed him. He was surprised with how happy and joyful the camp staff was towards him. Ranger greeted him right away with a hug and introduced Elliott to the Camp Director. The Camp Director played in the NHL for the Boston Bruins and made him feel welcomed.

After the first day, Elliott realized there was something different about the camp. The facilities were amazing, and the staff and other campers had a spirit of joy. It was weird and inviting all at the same time.

Elliott really didn't know anyone at the camp and the Camp Director knew this, so he tried to befriend Elliott by going out of his way to talk to him. Elliott appreciated the kind gesture and felt comfortable with him. As they were standing in the lobby together waiting for other players to arrive, Elliott decided to make some light conversation. He said to the Camp Director, "What is Richard's story?" It was more of a conversation starter since at the time Elliott didn't care about hearing a story, but he wanted to be friendly.

Elliott asked, "Do you know Ranger?"

The Camp Director smiled and said, "Oh yeah," I know Ranger. Why?"

Elliott said, "I'm just interested to hear his story." He had no idea what was about to hit him.

The Camp Director replied, "Well, Ranger Richard

played hockey at Army. Later in life, some of his closest friends and family gave him the name Ranger. He earned this nickname because the people around him embrace his heart. You see Ranger has an incredible heart for the Lord and went through a big sacrificial period, when he got a word from the Lord to sell his business and take his family on a five year, fifty-state tour of America, and build a hockey division of Fellowship of Christian Athletes (FCA Hockey).

"Before Ranger and his wife caught the vision of impacting the world of hockey through Jesus, one coach and one player at time, there was no FCA Hockey or North Star Christian Academy. Hey, just as a side note, I think about something Richard says all the time. The size of his heart was much more important than the size of body."

Elliott thought that was kind of weird. Anyway, the Camp Director went on to say that Richard was "tough, gritty, and aggressive when he played college hockey. He outworked everyone, with an aggressive edge. When he played at Army, he didn't get many penalties. For the most part he stayed out of the box and when he did get penalties, they were hard working penalties. He was ready to play a regular shift or two shifts per period. No matter what his ice time was, his teammates and coaches knew exactly what to expect from the Ranger, that's Richard."

Elliott laughed and said, "Oh, ok. Yeah, I get his name now," and they both chuckled.

PREPARING FOR THE GAME

The Camp Director went on to explain that Richard enjoyed physical play and knocking opponents off the puck. He was aggressive at net fronts. He loved to check, steal pucks, counterattack off turnovers, win personal battles, wall battles, and slot battles. He would outplay and out chirp anyone on the team and the opposing team. He would screen, pick, tip and dig for rebounds. He thrived on blocking shots. He was an energy forward with a never-say-die attitude who out-works, out-hits, out-smarts, out-thinks, out-skates, and out-shoots his opposition. He could change the course of the game through his intensity and raw determination—especially when the chips were down.

"The reason I am telling you this Elliott is because Ranger is a great man of God. I don't say that lightly, because he has done something here that is very, very special. You see Elliott, not much has changed since he stopped playing hockey. He has now channeled that same intensity in serving the Lord. During his playing days and now as the Director and Founder of FCA Hockey, Ranger has an unmatched intensity. As our leader here at NorthStar Christian Academy, not many people can keep up with his intensity and passion to communicate the Gospel of Jesus Christ. He loved hockey, but he loves Jesus even more! Ranger and his wife had a vision to see every hockey player receive Jesus as their Lord and Savior. When Ranger was driving all over the country and doing hockey clinics and camps, it didn't matter if there was one person or one hundred people there. They did the hockey camp or clinic and preached the Gospel of Jesus Christ."

Elliott was blown away and said, "Wait what did you just say?"

The Camp Director laughed and said, "And get this, Rangers wife homeschooled four kids and they had a newborn. And she did this in a 12-passenger van!"

Elliott had no words. He really didn't know what it meant to communicate or preach the Gospel, but he knew Ranger was 100% committed to this Jesus thing.

Elliott got to know almost everyone at that camp. The other players and staff were amazingly easy to talk with, so it was not hard to make friends. The competition was awesome, but the teaching of the Bible and about Jesus was overwhelming, especially on the last night of the camp. The Camp Director told his story of how he met Jesus. This was so strange to Elliott, and he didn't know what to do next. They talked about receiving Jesus as Lord and Savior, but he was just not ready to commit. The whole week at the camp was like trying to drink from a firehose. Elliott had too much thrown at him in a short period of time. Elliott could feel something good was planted in his heart, but he couldn't understand what it was or communicate what to do with it.

CHAPTER FOUR

THE NEXT DAY AT PRACTICE

JJ and Elliott unexpectedly met at the Zamboni doors again the next day. JJ had been standing there first. Elliott walked up behind JJ, who didn't turn to say hello because he was just watching the Mini Mites play. They had about four minutes left in their ice time and JJ had to jump on the Zamboni to clean the ice for the Hornets varsity team. Elliott didn't say "hi" or "hello" as JJ was staring at the Mini Mites. Elliott waited for about thirty seconds and said, "Low El." JJ responded, "Low El." Elliott had about fifteen minutes before he had to get dressed and be on the ice for practice, so he turned and walked back through the tunnel to his locker room. He was not looking forward to seeing Adrian, or even being in the same room to hear about last night's game.

GOOGLE HANGOUT

After practice, Kelly and Elliott were talking about their weekend. Kelly's team had swept Blake both games and won by four goals each game. They dominated the weekend. In fact, it was an easy weekend for Kelly. Most of her teammates were not challenged either. They didn't talk much about Kelly's games because there really wasn't much to say. Elliott was anxious and excited to talk about his game with Kelly.

Elliott said, "This weekend was really interesting, I went to the rink early to do my mental game prep and JJ sat down with me. Kelly was listening and walking around the house, but as soon as Elliott mentioned JJ, she did a double take.

She said, "Wait what? You talked to JJ?" Kelly walked briskly to her room, scrambling to find her journal.

Elliott said, "Yeah, I had the most interesting conversation with JJ. He talked to me about being aware of my emotions, empathy, and watching the emotions of the game. At first, I thought he was crazy, but after yesterday's game, I think he is a genius, like for real."

Kelly said, "Tell me more," as she reached down to the bottom of her dresser and pulled out her journal. It was under her three pairs of black Gym Shark training leggings. "There it is," she whispered.

Elliott said, "There what is?"

Kelly replied, "I found my journal where I am putting all of my JJ notes."

Elliott said, "Ok, well as I was saying…. I think JJ is more than a rink rat. He was talking to me about

NEXT DAY AT PRACTICE

High EI and Low EI."

"What is EI?" Kelly asked.

Elliott explained that EI stands for Emotional Intelligence. "An example of low EI might be if someone slashes you in the back of the leg and you thoughtlessly retaliate and slash back because you don't care about yourself or your team. JJ said when you do that, you are not in control of your emotions. He actually said that you are a slave to your emotions."

Kelly said, "Please, go on."

Elliott kept talking and said, "Yeah, so if someone slashes you in the back of the leg and you don't retaliate, that's called High EI. In this situation you are master to your emotions.

"At first, I was only sort of interested in what he was telling me. I was respectful and made a mental note of it, but now as I reflect back on our conversation, I think about Adrian tripping that player and when he couldn't get back to the net, they scored. And then a couple of minutes later, he chopped down the Blake player as he was skating through the crease. He chopped him down like he was cutting down a tree! I could see Adrian go Low EI, and remembered what JJ was telling me. I mean I could see the words over his head that read "Low EI" and the words were flashing over his head like a red neon sign… Low EI, Low EI… over and over again. I thought to myself, JJ was right. JJ had just talked to me about this and I was seeing it unfold right before my eyes. I was so blown away and then when Adrian tripped and hit his head on the boards, that was just disappointing and awful all in the same moment. Kelly, we need to talk to JJ about how to get out of that vicious cycle."

Kelly agreed and made some notes in her journal, including, *Build Awareness of High and Low EI.*

THE MASTER PLAN: COLLEGE AND PRO HOCKEY

Elliott and Kelly loved each other and for the most part everyone in the school loved them. It had never been done before, but school officials allowed Kelly to be Elliott's queen his senior year. Everyone could see they were a power couple. Elliott and Kelly were outstanding hockey players; they both scored a lot of goals and were great teammates.

Elliott declined the verbal offer to the Golden Gophers and accepted an NCAA Division 1 offer to Saint Cloud State. He wanted to be a Golden Gopher, but the situation just didn't work out. The community was excited for him. Elliott was a good student but didn't really care about any particular field of study, so he figured he would be a business major.

Kelly on the other hand, was excited about becoming a sports psychologist so she loved the idea of going to Saint Cloud. It was close to home and she was sure she could play hockey for them as well. Elliott was going to play one or two years of Juniors, then Kelly and he would meet at Saint Cloud, play hockey for the same school, get married during Elliott's 1st or 2nd year of pro. Elliott and Kelly knew he was headed to the NHL. As an NHL player he could help pay off all of Kelly's college debt, live in Edina and raise a family while Elliott played in the NHL. They were pretty sure Kelly was going to get a scholarship to play there as well. She was one of the best female players in the state, so getting an offer was going to happen. Since she wanted to pursue a Doctorate in Sports Psychology, they knew they were going to need extra money to pay for her schooling. They had talked about this almost every night. How she could help him with his playing as a sports psychologist and he could support her schooling. Kelly and her parents looked at the cost of advanced college degrees that Kelly would need to pursue her masters or doctorate to be a certified sports psychologist or certified mental performance coach. Kelly and Elliott had their path figured out and there wasn't anyone in either of their families who had any push back. They were both great students, great teammates, and they both had elite talents and abilities. They were a power couple, they loved each other, and nothing was going to derail their master plans.

KELLY'S SOPHOMORE YEAR

Kelly's team won the state championship again in her sophomore year, which was the second time she had won it. She led the team in scoring and assists in the game and for the second straight time, she led the team in scoring all year. She might be the first girl to win four state championships.

ELLIOTT'S SENIOR YEAR

Elliott's team also won the state championship. This is also Elliott's second year to win it. Elliott won as a Freshmen and now as a Senior and as a captain on the team. Elliott also was the team's leading scorer. Elliott had more goals than assists. Immediately after the state championship, Elliott was invited to skate in the United States Hockey League (USHL) with the Fargo Force.

THAT SUMMER BEFORE JUNIORS

Kelly and Elliott thought it was the coolest thing to label the next summer, the "summer before juniors." Kelly was going to be a junior in high school and Elliott was going to play his first year in Juniors with the Fargo Force. Elliott was super excited to play for Fargo. The USHL has teams all over America and most of the teams are west of the Mississippi River. Elliott was extremely grateful to be less than four hours from home. He could have played for any USHL team, but to be playing in Fargo was a blessing.

One Thursday night after practice, Kelly and Elliott saw JJ and he asked Elliott if he would like to go to a "College and Pro Camp" and train for a week. Elliott had never been to a "College and Pro Camp," so he was instantly excited. Elliott emphatically said, "YES!"

JJ said, "Ok great! I will let my buddy Ranger know you will be coming."

As JJ was leaving, Kelly looked at Elliott and whispered, "What about me? I want to go. Can I ask JJ if I can go? Or is it a boy's only camp?"

Elliott shrugged his shoulders and didn't know what to say. Kelly said, "Hey JJ, what about me, can I go?"

He looked back at her and said, "Sorry, Kelly. I think the girls camp is the week after the College and Pro Camp. The College and Pro camp is for boys only. I will check into it. Have a great night."

Within forty-eight hours, Ranger, the founder of FCA Hockey, called Elliott to say how happy he was that Elliott would be attending the College and Pro Camp at NorthStar Christian Academy in Alexandria, Minnesota, which was just two hours northwest of Edina, and Kelly would be going to the girls camp a week later. Kelly and Elliott were excited about their new adventures. Both Kelly and Elliott had passed Alexandria many times in their youth hockey careers playing games in Fargo. Though they were familiar with the drive, they had never stopped in Alexandria to play, which now they thought was kind of strange.

Both Elliott and Kelly were excited about the camp, but they didn't know what to expect. Kelly never talked with Ranger Richard, but she trusted Elliott's conversation with him. Elliott admitted that his phone call with Ranger was overwhelming because he talked fast, but with confidence. Elliott trusted JJ, so he trusted Ranger. Elliott was not sure why JJ invited him to the camp since he wasn't in college or a pro. Ranger talked about the talent, but also the faith aspect of the camp. Elliott was more interested in the competition of the camp and he didn't really think about the faith aspect of it at all.

Elliott arrived at camp and everyone welcomed him. He was surprised with how happy and joyful the camp staff was towards him. Ranger greeted him right away with a hug and introduced Elliott to the Camp Director. The Camp Director played in the NHL for the Boston Bruins and made him feel welcomed.

After the first day, Elliott realized there was something different about the camp. The facilities were amazing, and the staff and other campers had a spirit of joy. It was weird and inviting all at the same time.

Elliott really didn't know anyone at the camp and the Camp Director knew this, so he tried to befriend Elliott by going out of his way to talk to him. Elliott appreciated the kind gesture and felt comfortable with him. As they were standing in the lobby together waiting for other players to arrive, Elliott decided to make some light conversation. He said to the Camp Director, "What is Richard's story?" It was more of a conversation starter since at the time Elliott didn't care about hearing a story, but he wanted to be friendly.

Elliott asked, "Do you know Ranger?"

The Camp Director smiled and said, "Oh yeah," I know Ranger. Why?"

Elliott said, "I'm just interested to hear his story." He had no idea what was about to hit him.

The Camp Director replied, "Well, Ranger Richard played hockey at Army. Later in life, some of his closest friends and family gave him the name Ranger. He earned this nickname because the people around him embrace his heart. You see Ranger has an incredible heart for the Lord and went through a big sacrificial period, when he got a word from the Lord to sell his business and take his family on a five year, fifty-state tour of America, and build a hockey division of Fellowship of Christian Athletes (FCA Hockey).

"Before Ranger and his wife caught the vision of impacting the world of hockey through Jesus, one coach and one player at time, there was no FCA Hockey or North Star Christian Academy. Hey, just as a side note, I think about something Richard says all the time. The size of his heart was much more important than the size of body."

Elliott thought that was kind of weird. Anyway, the Camp Director went on to say that Richard was "tough, gritty, and aggressive when he played college hockey. He outworked everyone, with an aggressive edge. When he played at Army, he didn't get many penalties. For the most part he stayed out of the box and when he did get penalties, they were hard working penalties. He was ready to play a regular shift or two shifts per period. No matter what his ice time was, his teammates and coaches knew exactly what to expect from the Ranger, that's Richard."

Elliott laughed and said, "Oh, ok. Yeah, I get his name now," and they both chuckled.

The Camp Director went on to explain that Richard enjoyed physical play and knocking opponents off the puck. He was aggressive at net fronts. He loved to check, steal pucks, counterattack off turnovers, win personal battles, wall battles, and slot battles. He would outplay and out chirp anyone on the team and the opposing team. He would screen, pick, tip and dig for rebounds. He thrived on blocking shots. He was an energy forward with a never-say-die attitude who outworks, out-hits, out-smarts, out-thinks, out-skates, and out-shoots his opposition. He could change the course of the game through his intensity and raw determination—especially when the chips were down.

"The reason I am telling you this Elliott is because Ranger is a great man of God. I don't say that lightly, because he has done something here that is very, very special. You see Elliott, not much has changed since he stopped playing hockey. He has now channeled that same intensity in serving the Lord. During his playing days and now as the Director and Founder of FCA Hockey, Ranger has an unmatched intensity. As our leader here at North-Star Christian Academy, not many people can keep up with his intensity and passion to communicate the Gospel of Jesus Christ. He loved hockey, but he loves Jesus even more! Ranger and his wife had a vision to see every hockey player receive Jesus as their Lord and Savior. When Ranger was driving all over the country and doing hockey clinics and camps, it didn't matter if there was one person or one hundred people there. They did the hockey camp or clinic and preached the Gospel of Jesus Christ."

Elliott was blown away and said, "Wait what did you just say?"

The Camp Director laughed and said, "And get this, Rangers wife homeschooled four kids and they had a newborn. And she did this in a 12-passenger van!"

Elliott had no words. He really didn't know what it meant to communicate or preach the Gospel, but he knew Ranger was 100% committed to this Jesus thing.

Elliott got to know almost everyone at that camp. The other players and staff were amazingly easy to talk with, so it was not hard to make friends. The competition was awesome, but the teaching of the Bible and about Jesus was overwhelming, especially on the last night of the camp. The Camp Director told his story of how he met Jesus. This was so strange to Elliott, and he didn't know what to do next. They talked about receiving Jesus as Lord and Savior, but he was just not ready to commit. The whole week at the camp was like trying to drink from a firehose. Elliott had too much thrown at him in a short period of time. Elliott could feel something good was planted in his heart, but he couldn't understand what it was or communicate what to do with it.

CHAPTER FIVE

A NEW LIFE

Before Elliott got into the car, and was saying good-bye to his new friends, Ranger walked up and asked him, "How did it go this week?" Elliott gave him a big hug and said, "Thank you."

"What are you thanking me for? I'm just asking if you had a good time this week?" Ranger chuckled.

Elliott didn't really know why he said thank you and gave him a hug, but he knew it was the right thing to do, and it felt great to do it.

After Flliott hugged Ranger. Elliott said, "You know Ranger, yesterday I was completely overwhelmed, everything was really very new to me."
Elliott had never stuttered before in his life, but his eyes started to well up, tears were about to roll down his cheeks. Elliott said, "Wow!"

Ranger looked at him and gave him another hug and said, "It's a lot buddy."

Elliott replied, "Yeah, it is."

Ranger looked Elliott in the eyes and said, "Jesus loves you, Elliott. He knows everything about you and loves you. It sounds weird but if you let go, God will forgive your sin and you will be free from all your fears and anxieties."

Elliott responded, "How can I know for sure?"

Ranger said, "Because Jesus loves you and came to save you."

Tears started running down Elliott's face. He stuttered again and said "Yeah."

Ranger continued "Do you want to be free and accept Jesus into your heart today?" Elliott said "Yes I do" Elliott tried to look confidently into Rangers eyes, as he wiped the tears from his face.

Ranger said, "Do you believe that Jesus died on the cross for your sins?"

Elliott said, "Yes, I do."

Then Ranger told Elliott to repeat after him, "I believe that Jesus was the Son of God and that God sent Him to die on the cross for my sins. I believe Jesus is Lord, and today I want to accept Him into my heart."

After Elliott accepted Jesus into his heart, Ranger hugged and whispered into his ear, "Welcome to the Kingdom of God."

A NEW LIFE

Elliott had tears of joy as his stomach fluttered. He felt even more overwhelmed and more exhausted than yesterday, but for some weird reason he felt free. He felt a rapid fire of different feelings running through his head and heart. All new feelings that he had never experienced before. All he could do was cry.

As he was driving out of the parking lot, he called Kelly on his phone, two hands on the wheel of course, and as the sound of her voice echoed through the car's speaker system, Elliott continued to cry uncontrollably.

Kelly said, "Elliott are you ok? Elliott? Hello?"

After a minute or so, Elliott said, "I don't know what happened this week, but I feel like something has happened to me, and I can't explain it." Elliott gathered himself and said jokingly, "Kelly, you are next." She said, "what?" "You are next," he repeated. "You are going to love this place Kelly. You are in for something special."

Kelly said "Oh, ok. Well, what happened?"

Elliott said, "Well, the hockey was really good, and there were some great guys there. There were some really great players, but there was something else that hit me that I can't quite explain. I am looking forward to you coming here and experiencing it. I am sorry, but I need to go now. Can we talk later?"

Kelly said, "Ok, but I have so many questions."

Elliott said, "I know... I need to pay attention to the road."

Kelly said, "Elliott, are you ok?"

Elliott said, "Yes I am fine," and hung up the phone.

TRAINING TOGETHER

The day after Elliott returned from the camp in Alexandria. he wanted to work out with Kelly, because he wanted to spend as much time as possible with her. Their workouts were intense. Elliott had his buddies come over to work out with them. These were the same two guys who worked out with Elliott in the off season as they were growing up. Joseph and Timothy were fun guys and intense hard working fire breathers who were passionate about fitness. They loved to laugh and do crazy workout stunts, so it made the workouts go by fast. They also loved to eat, and they could eat a lot of food. Everyone looked forward to the workouts. They worked out together three or four days a week, sometimes even twice a day or late at night.

Part of their work out included skating, so Kelly and Elliott would do power skating together. They had a power skating instructor named Bambi, who was a big-time Christian. Bambi was a world champion figure skating instructor. She would constantly push Kelly and Elliott on their edge work, creating power drills that allowed them to trust their inside and outside edges. Kelly and Elliott had a love/hate relationship with Bambi. Bambi pushed them every time they stepped on the ice. Bambi worked with Edina boy's and girl's hockey teams throughout the year, so Kelly and Elliott had a very trusting relationship with her. Bambi always had a spirit of joy, peace, and patience on her heart. She was a world champion, so she had tremendous self-control. Kelly and Elliott never went to church, so they never really heard a message about Jesus being preached, but they heard that Bambi was a Christian through other people at the rink including JJ. Every time Kelly and Elliott were with Bambi, she was always positive and joyful. In passing, Kelly would sometimes say to Elliott, "If we ever become Christians, I think I want to be like Bambi who is always joyful. Elliott agreed and said, "Yeah I don't think anything bad ever happens to Bambi."

BAMBI

Bambi was one of five brothers and sisters who went into a foster home when it became clear their parents were not returning to them. Bambi and one of her brothers were adopted by an American mom and dad named Bill and Nancy who lived in Edina, Minnesota. They were praying for children just like Bambi and her brother. Later on, her brother wanted to be a missionary, so he went to Bible College at Moody Bible Institute in Chicago.

When Bill and Nancy brought Bambi back to the Edina community for the first time, she was four years old. Bill and Nancy knew they wanted her to get involved in sports. Nancy was a figure skater when she was growing up and had great memories of competing in skating competitions. Nancy had a loving relationship with her own mom and knew that competitive skating would teach Bambi how to succeed after a loss or failure. So, Nancy wanted Bambi to learn these valuable lessons, just like she had done years before.

Bambi was an amazing athlete and trainer, and though she was always encouraging to all the players, Bambi struggled with severe anxiety. She never felt as pretty as the other girls as she was growing up, so she proved her identity and self-worth through her skating and performance.

Her biological parents had been told they could make a lot of money in a short period of time harvesting palm oil back in their home in Indonesia, their home country. They were poor and uneducated, and so the idea consumed them. Out of love for their children and the idea of becoming amazing providers, they thought they could sacrifice a couple of months of being together to make money, and then come back and be set for the rest of their lives. After much deliberation, they decided to go, but when Bambi's parents arrived in Indonesia, their passports were taken, and they couldn't return home. They were forced to work in the fields and factories harvesting palm oil. They never returned to their children.

When Bambi was sixteen, she won the world championship in Palais Des Exposition in Nice, France. Her brother went to France with her and before they came home, Bambi having gone out with some teammates to celebrate, had a bad experience with vodka and orange juice. She got extremely drunk and passed out below a bridge. Somehow her best friend on the team found her after she received a weird text from Bambi. The text said, "Need ride home, under the bridge."

When her brother arrived, he immediately asked her if she wanted to receive Jesus as her Lord and Savior. At the time, Bambi wanted something in her life that was bigger than she was, She had the weight of the world on her shoulders at every corner of her life, so she said, "Yes" to her brother and to Jesus. That day changed her life and ever since then she wanted to make an impact on the lives of others. She used skating as a vehicle to help young figure skaters and hockey players. She felt blessed to be serving God this way and was passionate about the way she lived her life with integrity and account-ability. She was kind, joyful, and patient, and had incredible self-control. She used precision with her words and her body mechanics. She would often tell the people who were close to her that she was obsessed with helping athletes become better. Kelly and Elliott really enjoyed being around her. She was a bit preachy, but both Kelly and Elliott knew she loved Jesus and they respected that. They really appreciated that she shared her great motivational tips. She would say things like:

When thinking about life, remember no amount of guilt can change the past, and no amount of anxiety can change the future.

We will not fail today; we will find one hundred ways that don't work.

Your ability to perform is nothing compared to your ability to plan to perform.

She loved that one.

Bambi would start each of her sessions by saying, "I am obsessed with helping you become better, and I am fully present today. I pray you are as well."

Kelly and Elliott would laugh and make jokes about her motivational tips, not because they didn't think they were impactful, but because they didn't understand what they meant. They often said to each other, "I think we were just too young to understand" and then they would laugh. One thing Kelly and Elliott did understand was that Bambi was rescued by some people under amazing circumstances and that she was always ready to help them become better. In Bambi's mind she was helping God's children have a big impact in the Kingdom by helping the next generation to glorify the Lord with their talents and abilities. She felt honored to push her skaters beyond their own expectations because she knew they had more to give than they could think or imagine. She had experienced God and how much He had done for her. Kelly and Elliott could feel in her skating drills and on ice tempo that she had something special, but they were simply too young to understand her story.

One night after a private lesson with both Kelly and

Elliott, Bambi was extremely excited. She was more than her usual joyful, she was elated. She told Kelly and Elliott, "I have good news! My adoption agency has just approved me to adopt a North Korean teenage boy whose family was enslaved by forced labor. He needed a home in America. They chose me! I have prayed about this for years and now I can help just like my American parents helped me and my brother." Kelly and Elliott didn't really know what all this meant, but they could see that she was excited and that she was helping solve a big problem for a teenage boy in a similar way to what had happened to her.

Bambi was so excited that she asked Kelly and Elliott if they would pray with her. Elliott being a new Christian said, "Sure."

Kelly went along for the ride out of respect for Bambi, even though she had no idea what was about to happen.

Bambi settled herself and began to pray.

"Ok, Step 6. Pray about steps 1-5."

Kelly and Elliott looked up at each other with facial expressions that said, "What is about to happen?"

"Step 6?" they sort of whispered to each other.

Bambi continued, "Lord, today I am so thankful for Your Son Jesus. Today I am so thankful for the opportunity You have given me to serve Your children through power skating. I am thankful for the purpose and vision You have given me, and I am humbled for the strategy You have shown me. Every day, I have prayed for these steps and I am thankful You have given me spiritual eyes to see and spiritual ears to hear. I am thankful for the unique brand and communication You have given me in my work life and personal life."

Bambi paused as if she was listening to something or waiting for something. Elliott and Kelly were patient but felt awkward because they didn't know if the prayer was over or not. It was like Bambi was having a conversation with someone or something, but no one was there but them.

Bambi continued, "Lord, thank You for this child. Lord I understand that this new child in my life is not my child, but he is Your child, and I am just his ambassador for You. Lord, I am so thankful to be an ambassador over this child, and I ask You to give me strength and wisdom in the coming months and years to help this young man of God that you have so graciously allowed me to mentor. I promise to help him as You have helped me. I pray he will become a steward over Your purpose, vision, strategy, brand, and communication, and that I will continue to pray over these steps and my new son. I promise to make this a priority in my life as well as for all the children You put in my path. Thank you, Jesus. In Jesus' name. Amen.

Both Kelly and Elliott said, "Amen."

KELLY'S TURN

A week after Elliot came back from FCA camp in Alexandria Minnesota, Kelly made the trip to camp. Elliott didn't really talk more about his experience at the college and pro camp and Kelly didn't press him. She was nervous about going to the camp. Like Elliott, she received a warm reception. The Camp Director was nice, young, beautiful, and she played on the women's Olympic team, played Division I college hockey for the University of Alaska Anchorage and coached at Liberty University. Kelly could tell that she loved hockey and loved the Lord. She had the same spirit of joy as Bambi. There was no doubt Kelly felt welcomed and appreciated simply by the fact that someone young and knowledgeable about hockey was going to be at the camp. Like Elliott's experience, the players and coaching staff were amazing. On the last day of camp, the Camp Director told her story about how her identity was in hockey and how she went to a camp like this many years before and a player like her gave her story about how Jesus helped her in troubling times. And now here she was challenging this group.

Kelly felt like she was speaking directly to her but knew there were other players in the crowd. The Camp Director began to open the Bible and read the word of God and challenge her thought process, and her identity as a hockey player and she didn't like that feeling. Kelly was reflecting on her emotions and how they were up and down based upon her ice time, and her goals scored that week or game. Deep down Kelly felt like a fraud. She masked it well because she scored a lot of goals. She was happy one day because she scored two or three goals, and sad the next day because she didn't score. She realized she was not a master of her emotions.

The Camp Director went on to explain that God loves each of the girls in the room and that their sins were paid for by the blood of Jesus. If they wanted to shift their identity as a hockey player and have their identity in Jesus, they could receive that gift right now. All they had to do was say these words. "I confess my sin and believe that Jesus is my Lord and Savior. I believe that God raised Jesus from the dead and saved me from my sin."

Kelly was not as overwhelmed as Elliott had been. Kelly said to herself, "Ok wow, that's all I have to do? Say these words? No community service or Hail Mary's in a confession booth?" Kelly thought, "I could do that!" So, she followed the instructions of the Camp Director, repeated those words and committed her life to Jesus. She didn't really feel emotional because she was so matter of fact about it. After the camp was over, she was very appreciative of the time she spent with the staff and the Camp Director. She was looking forward to getting home and training with Elliott.

CHAPTER SIX

J. J.

Before the hockey season starts, JJ usually takes a couple of weeks here and there to ride his Harley motorcycle. He loves to take long road trips, usually back east. He has several friends on the east coast. It was the first week of August and he had just come back from Raleigh, North Carolina. It was a long, ten-day trip, but he enjoyed the ride and had many stops along the way. He spent two days in Raleigh and the rest of the time sightseeing. He took the longest route going there and the shortest one coming back and stopped many times to enjoy the scenery. He always appreciated nature and how God put it all together for people to enjoy.

When he got back, he decided he would drop into the rink and see what was happening. He pulled into his normal spot, the back of the rink near the Zamboni door. He walked in with his Harley chaps on and saw Kelly and Elliott having a private power skating session with Bambi. JJ was standing by the door as Kelly and Elliott came off the ice. They both stopped and said, "Hey JJ, we haven't seen you for a few days."

VISION WINS

Kelly and Elliott looked at each other at the same time. They both said at the exact same time, "We have some good news to share with you!"

JJ said, "What's up?"

Elliott continued, "Kelly and I went to that camp."

"What camp?" JJ said. "Oh yeah, the FCA Hockey camp? Right. How is Ranger?"

"Oh he is great," they both said.

"Well, we want to tell you that both Kelly and I accepted Jesus as our Lord and Savior."

JJ said, "This is amazing! I've been praying for both of you to have a good camp experience. Sounds like you had a GREAT camp!"

Kelly said, "Beyond amazing and we wanted to share the good news with you!"

"I'm so pumped for both of you," JJ said, and continued, "It's all coming together, just a few more steps. God has such a big vision for both of you."
Kelly and Elliott were happy that JJ was excited for them, but they were both kind of confused over the steps JJ was talking about.

"Hey, you two," JJ said, "Your futures are so bright I need sunglasses!"

JJ turned to walk back down the rink. The vibration from his Harley made his hands tingle after he had driven his motorcycle for more than three hours. He was looking forward to taking a nap and getting ready to start his week at the rink in the morning.

JJ looked around and said, "It's good to be back." He turned and started to walk towards them again. "Hey, you know what I love about both of you?"

Kelly and Elliott looked at each other and smiled and looked back at JJ. "What?" they both said at the same time and they all laughed.

JJ said, "I love that you both live the practice and train with intent and purpose." There was an awkward silence and Kelly said, "Is this some type of code again? You know JJ, Elliott and I talk about your messages all the time. Let's see what your first message to Elliott was."

Elliott stood there with one hand on his hockey stick, legs crossed slightly, leaning on his hockey stick with one hand.

He said, "If I don't have a plan to win, then I plan to lose." Kelly opened her eyes wide and said," Step 1: Vision: What is the future I am fighting for? The last one you talked to me about that I wrote in my journal was Step 2: High and Low EI."

Elliott corrected her, "It was to build awareness of high and low EI."

"That's right," Kelly said, and continued, "What do you mean by live the practice, train with intent and purpose?"

JJ said, "You two are awesome! This is why you are a power couple. You figure things out really fast. Listen, I just came back from a long trip. I will meet up with you later and explain it all to you."

Kelly protested, "Wait, what do you mean explain it all to us? Do you mean explain 'live the practice, train with intent and purpose' or is there more?"

She continued as JJ started to walk away.

 "JJ! Come on, is there more, more, or just more from this? Come on JJ all your stuff is always dead on. Please JJ."

JJ replied, "I will give it ALL to you next week. Ok. Next year is a big year for both of you and I promise I will unload the details, promise!"

"By the way, I am super excited you have found Jesus and your purpose," JJ said.

They smiled in agreement and walked towards the tunnel and into their respective locker rooms behind the rink. JJ turned and walked down the boards checking out the ice surface, paying close attention to the level of the ice, its smoothness, and the edges around the boards specifically below the yellow board where the ice meets the boards. JJ walked towards the Zamboni room.

That night when Kelly got home, she wrote in her journal:

Step 1: Purpose: Jesus
   Mental toughness: Live the practice, train with intent, and purpose.

JJ DIES

It was a normal school day for Kelly and for the rest of the Edina community. That is, it was a normal day until the students arrived at the school and there were three firetrucks and two ambulances and countless police cars. Elliott had graduated back in May, so he didn't have to go to school and the next week he was leaving to report to the main campus in Fargo. He wanted to spend as much time as possible with Kelly, so he decided to drop her off and pick her up from school.

Elliott will never forget that first week of school, September 10th. That day is forever etched in his memory. The feeling in the air was confusion, uncertainty, and curiosity as he parked his car and walked Kelly up through the parking lot, holding her hand.

"Man, I love her"... he was thinking, despite the chaos around them. He realized it was a normal school day except he wasn't going to school. That was kind of weird. As they were walking through the parking lot, they saw the police cars and a parade of people walking towards the Braemer Rink. Braemer had three rinks under one roof and a big parking lot. They didn't know what was happening, but it was huge, whatever it was. They kind of ignored it until they walked up to the high school doors.

Then they heard the words, "JJ died."

Kelly and Elliott looked at each other like, "What?" They couldn't believe what they were hearing, so they followed the kids who were headed out of the school, walking fast, almost running over to the rink.

"We arrived at the rink," Elliott remembered, "and there was yellow tape around the rink. The tape read, 'Police Line - Do Not Cross,' and we could see there was a fire truck parked at the front of the rink and two firetrucks and two ambulances parked back by the rink near the Zamboni door. A crowd was gathering as the school principal came out with one of those blue and white thunder power bull horns and said, 'Students, we have experienced a great tragedy today. We don't have any details right now, so we are asking you to please go back to the high school and attend your classes. We will keep you informed and updated as we know more.'

Kelly said, "Tragedy, oh my God, what has happened?" A senior in her math class confirmed that JJ had died.

An overwhelming sense of emotions came over Elliott who was trying to hold it in and did, until his eyes began to swell as tears rushed down his face. He turned away from Kelly so she could not see him, but she knew what was happening. He looked at her and she burst into tears and put her head on his shoulder. Elliott couldn't remember exactly what he said to her because everything became a complete blur.

THAT EVENING

Elliott continued, "I can't remember the exact time, but later that day, I picked Kelly up from school early. She was an emotional mess and quite honestly, I was still a mess too. I thought I was doing a good job of masking my emotions. On the outside, I appeared calm, but inside, I felt like Kelly looked. It was the first time in both of our lives that someone close to us had died.

"That evening the local news reported that long-time Zamboni driver Jeremiah James, better known as JJ to the Edina community, died while working underneath the ice resurfacing machine." My whole family was glued to the TV. The reporter on the local Fox affiliate went on to say that this was horrific news for our community. "I am sad to report that JJ was discovered underneath an ice resurfacing machine. It is not clear how he ended up under the machine outside of Braemar Arena. The Edina Police and Occupational Health and Safety (OHS) officials are investigating the tragic workplace death. OHS said it could not provide any additional details at this time as the investigation is ongoing."
The reporter paused in sadness and cut to a video outside the rink, where Kelly and Elliott had been

standing earlier in the day. It was an all too famil-iar scene as they had walked past the front doors a million times. It was like home to them, and now they were watching the Athletic Director and Head Coach of the men's hockey team sadly express, *"I don't know what to say."*

His eyes were red, and you could see he was upset and emotional.

"It's horrific, JJ was part of our community and we loved him. It will take us some time to recover from this incredible loss. This was not a good day for our Hornets. We have never suffered a big loss like this, but I know this community will honor JJ and nev-er forget the impact he has made on each of us." Coach lowered his head and walked off camera.

The screen cut back to the reporter in the local Fox newsroom. She quietly said, "OHS said it had a call from police on its accident-reporting line early today. The impact of a workplace fatality is felt by family, friends, and co-workers, and resonates with all the people in the hockey and greater Edina community. We offer our deepest condolences to the family."

The news went to an annoying local car dealership commercial. Elliott's dad abruptly turned off the television.

JJ EULOGY
When Kelly and Elliott arrived at the funeral home,

it was packed with cars. They saw all the different license plates and realized some people had driven a long way to get here, and some had even flown here. They were surprised so many people were here for JJ's funeral. There were too many people to walk across the funeral home, so they sat down, four rows behind the first row of seats on the left side.

Two people spoke during the service: JJ's BFF and his brother, Edward.

Elliott didn't remember the BFF's actual name because he never said his name. He just said he was JJ's BFF. He was very emotional and passionate about his relationship with JJ. When he first walked up to the pulpit, he looked familiar, and after he was done talking, Elliott realized the man had coached at the FCA Hockey camp in Minnesota. Elliott loved that camp and was very interested in what the coach had to say.

JJ's BFF said...

JJ and I spoke often about Jesus and our relationship with Him. He knew where he was going, and I knew him well enough to know that his last request would be that I share his faith and certainty with you. If any of you are worried about your eternity, you might need to hear this today.

"God wrote an autobiography. We call it The Holy Bible, His Word, His testimony. He originally gave this Word to His chosen people, and they called it the Law. The

Law described the statutes and standards of God that defined God's perfect truth, perfect nature and perfect thoughts and actions. Now in possessing such a Law, God wanted men to realize that no man could be justified in keeping this Law; no matter how earnestly that man tried to keep the perfect demands. Rather than justification, this Law was meant to teach man more about his frailties and failings than about his triumphs or successes. This Law held a standard of God; a standard that no man could reach.

Now God gave His chosen people a strange lesson to practice, over and over again, until the time would come when no more practice was needed. It was an odd practice of vicarious atonement. It involved an offering of a spotless, innocent lamb as a substitutional appeasement for the judgment of man's failure against the perfect, unattainable standards of the Law of God.

That Lamb was known as the Passover Lamb because the judgment of God mercifully passed over all those who put their faith in the blood of that Spotless Lamb rather than on the pride of their own achievement.

JJ wants you to know that he put all of his faith in Jesus, the Lamb that God provided so no further Passover lambs would ever need to be offered again. JJ wants you to know that, just as the veil of the Temple was torn when the Lamb willingly laid Himself on the altar of the cross, he also was cut loose and set free by a circumcision of the heart. JJ wants you to know that he did nothing, nothing at all, to earn or deserve the gift of the Lamb. He only needed to accept it and believe.

Now, have you ever wondered if Abraham was crazy when he placed Isaac on the altar? Was he a mad man, wanting to show a religious devotion so insane that he would sacrifice his child in some crazy ceremony demanded by a harsh and unloving God? God had promised Abraham that through the seed of Isaac many great leaders and a nation of people would come. When God asked Abraham to offer Isaac as a sacrifice, Isaac had no son. He had no "seed" to fulfill the promise of God, and yet Abraham so trusted and believed in the promises of God that he had no fear of offering Isaac on that altar. Abraham knew somehow God would resurrect, restore, or prevent the death of Isaac so that Isaac's seed would be born, and God's promises would be fulfilled. As many of you know, JJ had the faith of Abraham, a faith upon which he would trust his own life and the life of his own son and his grandson.

JJ was not a man of great material wealth, and yet he was a very rich man. JJ lived his life wealthy in the grace he had been given, the unsearchable riches of Jesus Christ, and so now he is with Jesus in glory. JJ loved excellence and wanted to glorify the Lord with his talents and abilities and wanted to help other people do the same. If he were here now, he would want you to do the same, and he would encourage you. I pray that you too can live a life of fulfillment as JJ did. He would expect nothing less from us all.

He finished with the two words "vision wins." Elliott was blown away by those words because he had heard them before. JJ said those words to him in their first real conversation together. JJ's BFF didn't emphasize those words. He actually said them under his breath as he closed his notebook and walked off the funeral home stage.

After a few minutes, an older man stood up and walked to the front of the funeral home with a guitar. He stepped up to the front of the stage and quietly reached the podium.

He said, "I am JJ's older brother Edward." He purposefully looked east, west, north and south around at the crowd of people. There wasn't an empty seat, and families were standing by the wall and sitting on folding chairs that were packed around the room. People still filed in as Edward began to speak.

JJ was a man who understood unifying people and what it meant to strive for excellence. He loved the Lord and dedicated his life to pursuing his God-given talents. I didn't think he really liked helping people, but maybe he did. Everyone here says he did, and it looks like he did a lot of it. You are all a testimony of how he helped people understand their purpose and identity.

Edward paused and smirked as if he knew something different about his little brother, a deeper connection. *Yes, I am the big brother who beat up his little brother; I am not going to lie. I enjoyed teasing him, stripping him down naked and throwing him outside and locking the doors to the house so he couldn't get back in.* (The crowd strangely laughed.) *Yeah, I did that, but I also gave him back his own hockey card collection that I had taken from him ten years before.*

Everyone laughed and appreciated the levity. Edward paused and said, *Seriously,* and paused again as a tear went down his face. *My little brother was a mentor to me. He was a great example of what I wanted to do with my life. He had integrity in his marriage. He was only married once. His wife was wonderful, and their relationship was amazing. Their kids are something special too. I love that about my brother. I looked up to him and he held me accountable when I needed it. He helped me be accountable by the life he led. He was an overachiever, and his marriage and his kids were a reflection of him. He did his best to be a reflection of Christ. I can remember when he got accepted for his Sport and Performance Doctorate and he posted his acceptance letter on Facebook. My comment which I later regretted was, "Will you please stop achieving?" I didn't really understand what he did for hockey players, but I see that his impact was far and wide.*

As you all know, or maybe you don't know, JJ figured out a lot of life lessons that you and I couldn't. He was a USAF Veteran. He figured out how to serve his country and play hockey in Germany. He figured out how to get paid to play hockey and get paid by the government. He was a genius in a way. I can't believe

I just said that! (He smiled and went on.) As he was living in Germany, he also figured out how to get his Business degree and get it paid for by the government. After he left Germany, with a beautiful, amazing God-fearing woman as his soul mate, he started a marketing company. He did very well with his marketing company, working with ministries and leaders all around the world. I respect the fact that he wanted to retire and hang around the rink living a stress-free life. He absolutely loved hockey. He loved this community, the Hornets games, the crowds, the youth, and everything the hockey community represents.

He coached hockey at the youth, junior or college level, so he experienced hockey parents and the drama that often comes with it. We didn't talk every day, but we were close. He helped me on what I called "miracle weekend.' I was struggling at the time with depression and he raised a lot of money and organized a lot of people to come to my house and help me fix it up. I am still blown away when I think about it. If he were here, he would probably say, "If it were not for the grace of God, there go I." He didn't like to take credit for things. He loved to give God all the Glory. JJ was a man of God that wanted to have his identity in Christ and wanted others to experience that victory. As I look around this funeral home, I can see that JJ had great people in his life, and that his life's work is a reflection of the fruit of the Spirit. I can see that everyone here is the fruit of his spirit and time on earth. JJ understood his identity was not in his ability to play or coach hockey, but his identity was in his love of Christ.

J. J.

Thank you for joining me today. I can see a lot of you drove a great distance or flew to get here. My family and I are very appreciative of your support.

As Edward looked around the funeral home, he could feel the sense of love, peace, kindness and goodness in the hearts and minds of everyone in the room.

Edward said, "Please join me as we celebrate JJ going home."

Edward picked up his guitar and sang, "Celebrate Me Home" by Ruben Studdard.

DRIVING HOME

Elliott and Kelly were trying to hold it together in the funeral home. Everyone was a mess, but they went to their car without showing too much emotion. Once they got in and closed both their doors, they looked at each other and started to cry uncontrollably. It was the first time Elliott cried in front of Kelly. In fact, she could not remember any time she ever saw Elliott cry. After several minutes of crying and composing themselves, Kelly had make-up all over her face, and they only had one tissue between them, so Elliott had Kelly's makeup on his nose and cheeks as they were sharing the same tissue.

Once they composed themselves, they looked at each other and said, "JJ was a Doctor and a coach?" They were both astonished and realized they really didn't know anything about JJ. They thought he was a lonely old Zamboni driver. Kelly looked at Elliott after blowing her nose on the same wet and used tissue and said, "What did we take for granted all those years?"

Elliott had that unsettling feeling again, the one he experienced when JJ said if he didn't have a plan, then he was planning to fail. There was something more in Elliott's mind and spirit, but he didn't know what it was or how he was supposed to get there. As they were driving away from the funeral home, Elliott glanced back through the rearview mirror and saw Ranger and his family leaving the funeral home. He was pleased that Ranger was there.

Elliott didn't say anything to Kelly but having Ranger there confirmed to Elliott that JJ was an impact player in many significant people's minds and hearts. Up until the funeral, JJ's words and conversations had confused Elliott more than they enlightened him. Seconds after he saw Ranger Richard in his rearview mirror, he began to instantly process and rethink the moments he spent with JJ. Elliott was overwhelmed.

As they drove home, they both were unfocused. They felt fragile and vulnerable over losing their mentor and friend.

CHAPTER SEVEN

OPENING NIGHT AT EDINA

It was opening night for the Hornets, and they honored JJ by putting stickers on their helmets. The stickers were one inch in diameter, white, with green JJ letters. Both the boy's and girl's teams, JV and Varsity put the stickers on their helmets. The youth hockey at Edina wore the stickers as well. After the video played on the jumbotron, the scoreboard announcer said, "Let's all bow our heads in a moment of silence."

This was Kelly's Junior year opening night, and she was inspired by the Edina community and their support for JJ. She had a natural hat trick that night, scoring three goals in a row and had three assists. Six points. They won seven to two.

At the first of the year, Kelly was expecting many D1 offers. She was excited about her future as a collegiate athlete. She was more than likely going to become the first hockey player to win four straight state championships. She smashed all scoring records in previous years, and she was beloved by her teammates and the Edina community. This year she was a Co-Captain and there was no doubt that next year she would be the captain of this team for her senior year.

KELLY WINS 4 STRAIGHT

Kelly was a senior now and did something very few high school hockey players in the world have ever done in their playing careers. Kelly had won three state championships in a row. Every week she had NCAA Division I schools offering her full ride scholarships. She had letters and many phone calls throughout the week of her senior year and now she was about to win her 4th State Championship.

3-2-1 the crowd went wild!

The spirit of joy and excitement overcame Kelly as she heard the buzzer go off and the crowd chant 3-2-1. Gloves, helmets, and sticks went up in the air. Kelly finished her senior year as a four-time high school hockey champion in the Xcel Energy Center in Minneapolis, Minnesota. Kelly would be the most decorated and celebrated female hockey player in Minnesota high school hockey history. Her identity in hockey was cemented for the rest of her life.

The next couple of weeks created amazing moments in Kelly's life. She had multiple media interviews and accepted a full ride scholarship to St. Cloud State. She was so excited to be joining Elliott at St Cloud. She had every Division I NCAA hockey program in the country wanting her to attend their school. Her decision was easy, she wanted to be with her high school sweetheart.

NHL DRAFT NIGHT

The Edina community was inspired, and local youth hockey was empowered with Kelly and Elliott having so much success. The surrounding communities were happy for the local area and what their success did for the state of Minnesota hockey but there were some people who were very jealous of Edina. Elliott getting drafted was another reason to stir their jealousy. Elliott hoped they would become better, not bitter.

Elliott was beyond excited about the NHL Draft. Everyone in the Edina community was excited to see what was going to happen. There was endless buzz in all of the surrounding cities of Edina. The morning before Elliott left to go to the Draft hosted at the American Airlines Center in Dallas Texas, the local FOX affiliate interviewed him. From the Arden Park pond hockey shack, the local Edina kids were inspired by his words:

"I am super excited about the Draft. It is a big event and something every kid who plays hockey wants to experience. I spoke to about twenty teams at the NHL combined, and four teams want to meet with me later today once I get to Dallas. At this point, I just hope to move forward so my dream of getting drafted becomes a reality."

LATER THAT NIGHT

Elliott was nervous. He knew he was going to get drafted, he just did not know when or what team was going to select him. That morning he had talks with the general managers from the Carolina Hurricanes, Dallas Stars, Phoenix Coyotes, and the Minnesota Wild.

As he sat there in the lower bowl of the stadium chewing his nails trying to remain calm, cool and collected, he found himself going between talking with Kelly, holding her hand, chewing his fingers, and talking to his dad. Time seemed to have stopped as teams were starting to make their selections. Ironically, the teams were selecting players who were sitting in the same section and row as Elliott. This didn't help Elliott's anxiety. Time seemed to stop, but it sped up real fast when he heard these words:

And the Carolina Hurricanes select as their 25th overall choice in this year's draft: Elliott Podofski.

Elliott stood up and hugged his parents with tears running down his face and said, "Mom and Dad, thank you. I love you so much." Elliott had an immediate flash back from his pond hockey days, as he was walking down the stairs from the stadium. His phone was buzzing with phone calls and text messages. He ignored his phone as he walked towards the stage.

Just like Kelly, Elliott's identity as a hockey player was now forever cemented into the Edina community. He would become a hero for other Hornets players in the Edina youth hockey world. Elliott was on his way.

Elliott landed at MSP Airport Terminal one, and the same FOX affiliate reporter was there waiting for him, along with other people from the local community. He gladly did the interviews.

"It was fun hearing my name being called on the big stage. All things considered; the Draft went by pretty quickly. My favorite part was being able to sit in the Dallas Stars suite in the arena wearing my own NHL Draft jersey with my Mom and Dad sitting next to me. They were such a huge part of me getting drafted and being able to share the moment with them was the best part, after hearing my name getting called."

Elliott moved through the crowd and signed some autographs. He jumped into his dad's Jeep and went home. His house was only about fifteen minutes from the airport. He went to his room and passed out. He was mentally exhausted from the excitement, the interviews, and the travel.

ELLIOTT IN JUNIORS

Elliott had two successful years playing for the Fargo Force in Fargo, North Dakota. The coaching staff at St. Cloud State had not changed and his verbal offer for a full ride scholarship was still available to him. After he made a commitment, other Division One and Ivy league schools stopped recruiting him. The SCS coaching staff was excited about having Elliott on their roster. Elliott was smart, fast and had a heavy shot. He led his Junior team in scoring, and he was a vocal leader on and off the ice. His team-mates and coaches respected him. Elliott's time in Fargo allowed him to get stronger, mentally and physically, and learn more about his positioning in the defensive zone. Most importantly, he became more experienced and prepared himself for longer seasons. That first year he played seventy-five games, including playoffs.

THE DAY

"Mary have you seen my Huskies hat?" Elliott's dad, Steve, said shouting from his bedroom as Mary, Elliott's mom was in the kitchen putting away the dishes. Mary wouldn't leave her kitchen dirty when they traveled. They didn't travel much but when they did, she wanted to come home to a clean house.

Steve walked out of the bedroom and into the kitchen. "Honey have you seen my new college hat? I have been looking all over for it."

Mary replied, "It's in your closet on the shelf above the safe."

"Ok, awesome." He gave her a kiss on the neck and a big bear hug, lifting her off the ground.

"Steve!" Mary exclaimed.

Steve was so excited. "Do you know how long we have been waiting for this night? This is one single step, a giant leap for mankind! Our son is about to play

Division One College hockey on a full ride scholarship."

As he was walking away, Steve said, "We are one step closer to the NHL!" Mary followed him to the bedroom to pack after she put her last dish in the cupboard.

"Steve," said Mary, "Remember, we love our son because he is our son and he is going to do great things with his life, not just because of his hockey accomplishments, great as they are and will be."

Steve said, "I know, I know, but honey, tonight our son will play D1 hockey. Do you know how long he has been dreaming of this moment? I can remember when Kelly and Elliott and their gang of pond hockey buddies were talking about playing for the Gophers and then going on to the NHL. My earliest memory is like he was five or six years old. Do you remember that honey? I mean our son has been drafted into the NHL, what an honor! I mean this is just the beginning, wow, that is really strange to think about how this is just the beginning of his career, but you know it's a major milestone. Tonight, marks a major milestone."

Steve was nervously walking around the bedroom getting his clothes together, throwing pants, shirts, and socks into his small luggage bag. Mary left the bedroom to go to the laundry room which was on the other side of the house.

Steve looked up and said, "Honey? Honey? Where did you go?"

"I am over here, Steve," Mary replied as she sorted and folded Steve's clothes that he had no idea he was going to wear.

Steve began to walk towards the laundry room. "Mary, what time is Kelly coming over, again?

Steve, Mary, and both of Kelly's parents, Karen and Dave were carpooling to St Cloud. Although it was just under four hours, the families were meeting ninety minutes early. When they all talked about the schedule, they agreed it was a cushion in case they hit some traffic coming out of the cities. But deep down they were all too excited to stay at home.

Mary said, "They are coming over after lunch and we are leaving around 1:00."

The Huskies were playing Denver twice this weekend. Tonight, is their home opener at the Herb Brooks Arena in Saint Cloud Minnesota.

There were several friends and family members, former teammates and fans from the community coming to see Elliott play tonight, but they were not leaving that early. The schedule worked out great. Kelly didn't have any games this week. It was a rare weekend that she was not playing two or three games. Kelly was super excited to see Elliott play. She realized it was unusual that she was not playing, like she was supposed to be there.

OPENING NIGHT AT EDINA

PUCK DROP

They arrived at the rink at 5:45 PM, and puck drop was at 7:05 PM. The doors didn't open until 6:00 PM. There were hundreds of people shuffling into the lobby of the rink, and the lobby was amazingly decorated in red and white. You could feel the success of the building and the presence of the Huskies nation. Elliott had left tickets for everyone at the will call window. Steve was leading the carpool team to the front of the will call window. They comfortably got their seats, soaking in the building, the glass, the student body, and the excitement.

It didn't feel strange that they didn't see green and white everywhere as they were accustomed to seeing back in Edina. Instead, it felt new and exciting for them. This wasn't Kelly's first time in the Herb Brooks Arena. She accepted her verbal offer for college the week before. She could have gone to any school in the country but chose SCS because she wanted to share her life with Elliott. She was the top recruit on every D1 list in the nation. SCS didn't have to do too much recruiting to get her.

All they had to do was be friendly and welcome her with open arms. Her grades were outstanding, and she was the only female athlete to win four state championships. She smashed all high school point records by fifty points, twenty-seven goals and twenty-three assists. The Edina community and the state of Minnesota hockey officials and fans contend there will never be another female athlete that will beat her scoring record.

VISION WINS

The rink is starting to fill up. The student section, youth players, alumni and people from the community are finding their seats. The lights come up and the visiting team comes out for warmups. Both team equipment managers throw a couple dozen pucks on the ice. The Denver players start to come out, and the fans start booing. As the last Denver player comes out of the tunnel and jumps onto the ice, snapping his helmet and quickly catching a random puck, the music changes and the Saint Cloud State Huskies team comes running out onto the ice. They didn't look disheveled. They looked organized and fast, and one after another they came running onto the ice. Steve, Mary, Karen, Dave and Kelly were looking for number eighteen, and there he was the twelfth player to come flying out on the ice. Kelly said, "There he is," and Mary and Steve said almost together, "I see him." They were all standing and watching the warmups, and then sat down and watched the game as if they had not been to a million games before. The idea of Elliott being a Huskie and wearing number eighteen was settling in.

NATIONAL ANTHEM

Both teams lined up on their respective goal lines. First, the announcer introduced the visiting team's starting lineup to the quiet home team crowd. Many of the SC students held up newspapers, appearing bored and disinterested in what was happening. Steve, Mary, Karen and Dave had never seen this before and they got a chuckle out of it and deep down, they loved it.

As the announcer said, "And now the starting lineup for your Huskies," the place erupted as the background music changed and the spotlight shined on each team member as their numbers and names were called. Then the light changed again, but this time it was on Elliott. Once again, the booming voice of the announcer introduced number eighteen, Elliott Podofski, and the place went crazy just like the other players but this time Kelly, Steve, Mary, Karen, and Dave looked at each other at the exact same time and Kelly said, "Wait what? Is he starting? He told me on our drive up that he thought he might only see three or four minutes of ice time. How the heck did he break into the lineup?"

This was a scene the family had witnessed a million times during the National Anthem. Elliott was going through his mental preparation routine right in front of them. Elliott had the same body mechanics, the same sequence and cadence with his feet and head moving in his predetermined pattern, because he was laser focused on the 'here and now.' He was amazingly comfortable with his mental state.

14 SECONDS LATER

The puck dropped. Elliott won the face-off and the puck sailed back to his defenseman. At the same time Elliott won the face-off to the right-handed defenseman, the left-handed left winger raced to the board, just over the center ice line. The defenseman made a hard crisp pass to the winger only to lightly touch the puck, so that icing would not be called, but to leave most of the momentum on the puck so that it would travel into Denver's defensive zone. Kelly, Steve, Mary, Karen, and Dave could see that it was a routine play.

Elliott took off to chase down the puck into the corner. He was catching up to the defenseman, closing in on him and the puck. He was not quite even with him, when they both headed to the boards, just a few feet ahead of them.

Elliott was a half-step behind the defenseman. With two hands on his stick, he awkwardly attempted to hit his opponent. The hit didn't land the way he thought it would, and with his own momentum behind him, Elliott tripped. As he fell, he crashed into the boards, smacking his head and helmet into the boards. He landed on the ice after his fall; his body was limp, almost lifeless.

The referee blew his whistle and a hush fell over the entire stadium. Everyone in the crowd and on the ice held their breath. The only sound in the stadium was the shuffle of people rising out of their seats, waiting to see #18 get back up. The sounds of the bottom of the chairs smacking the tops of the seats as people stood up echoed in an inconsistent wave across the stadium.

Kelly, Steve, Mary, Karen, and Dave jumped to their feet. Their hearts were beating fast. They had their hands over their mouths and noses, and their countenances dropped in shock and fear. Steve felt dizzy and overwhelmed, so he sat back down, but never took his eyes off Elliott, lying motionless on the ice.

For everyone else in the crowd, they were all thinking, hoping, praying that #18 would stand back up. But experienced fans and players were all thinking about the way his body hit the boards, and how he fell to the ice, limp and lifeless, it didn't look like he could get up on his own.

It had only been thirty seconds since the crash into the wall, but it felt like hours as they waited to see movement. Two trainers and the Assistant Coach immediately ran out onto the ice. Elliott didn't move. There was no movement from his feet or body. A couple of minutes later the double doors opened, where the Zamboni is parked, and two paramedics walked out with the ambulance stretcher, one on either side. There was a hush in the building.

Elliott hoarsely whispered, "Can someone get my dad?" When he spoke, it sounded like every breath, every word was exhausting, taking all his energy. As his body lay paralyzed on the cold ice, he couldn't feel anything. The only thing Elliott could do was move his mouth.

The Assistant Coach said, "What did you say, Elliott?" Elliott whispered again, "Can someone get my dad?"

Meanwhile, Steve had pushed through the crowd to get to his son. He was inches from the Zamboni door, and racing to be at his son's side. Once on the ice, he approached Elliott, leaned over and said, "Elliott, what's happening?"

"Dad," Elliott said, his voice weak, "Dad I'm scared, I think I'm in big trouble. I can't feel anything below my neck, and it hurts really bad."

Steve wanted to be positive and say the right thing to him, but he just couldn't come up with any words. Steve was mentally and emotionally in shock and completely depleted. He stood up and looked up to the top of the arena, searching for words, a higher power, something other than this fear which gripped him to the point where he could barely breathe. He didn't know what to think or do and then he heard, "Dad" …

Steve bent over again and said "Yes, son. What is it?"

Elliott whispered again, "Can you come down here by my side?"

Steve got on his hands and knees and looked him straight in the eye and Elliott said "Dad, I made it, I made it Dad."

Steve responded, "Yes you did son, yes you did. We are all so proud of you." Then Steve burst into tears before telling the paramedics that we need to get him out of here.

After securing his head and body with restraints, the

medical team and trainers picked Elliott up off the ice, carefully put him on a stretcher and wheeled him out of the rink and into the ambulance and then they rushed him to the local hospital.

After about ten hours, the ER surgeon came out to give the family the bad news. Elliott had cracked his fourth and fifth vertebrae, rendering him limited use in his arms and legs. He was stabilized with restraints so as not to further injure himself. He was in an induced coma and on a ventilator to keep him breathing.

He spent the next four months doing physical and occupational therapy, but most of the time he was laying in the hospital bed, he had time to think and pray about his future. Several times throughout the week Kelly would come and visit. Hockey was never too far from his mind. He received letters almost daily from the local Edina community and a parade of hockey royalty came to see him. The reality of Elliott not walking again was gaining traction, but somewhere in all the despair as his dream died, a new vision was starting to emerge.

CHAPTER EIGHT

EVERYTHING HAS CHANGED

Weeks and months, after the accident, several people reached out to Elliott's parents. Steve and Mary were very appreciative but as the calls kept coming, they were also growing weary of telling the same story over and over without new news or hope. One of the concerned phone calls came from Ranger who offered prayers and assistance to Steve and Mary. In fact, Ranger was one of the few who asked about Kelly and her emotional state. Steve, who was on the phone with Ranger, was amazed that Ranger asked about Kelly. Ranger offered to pray for the family, and Elliott and Kelly and Steve gratefully accepted.

Before Ranger prayed with Steve, he asked Steve if he could talk to Elliott the next day, and Steve said that he thought that would be great!

Ranger prayed and Steve could feel the stress and anxiety lift from his shoulders. Steve thanked Ranger and they hung up.

THE NEXT DAY
"Hey Ranger," said Elliott.

"Hey buddy, how are you holding up?" Ranger asked.

Elliott replied. "Oh you know, living the dream."

Ranger said, "The reason for my call today is that I want to tell you that nothing has changed."

Ranger paused as an uncomfortable amount of time passed and patiently waited for Elliott's response. Ranger wanted to make sure Elliott understood the foundation of his message before he moved on.

"No, Ranger. Everything has changed!" sighed Elliott.

Ranger quickly jumped in and said, "I wanted to call you and tell you that today is no different than any other day because God loves you, regardless of your ability to play hockey. You see the Old Testament was about how we serve God through our sacrifices, and in the New Testament God sent his only Son Jesus to die for our sins, so you don't have to do anything to have a relationship with Him. All you and I need to do is love Him and glorify Him. You see the purpose and passions in your heart will be on red alert in the coming days."

Elliott stopped him and said, "What do you mean, red alert?"

Ranger replied, "What I mean is that you are going to challenge your own identity now that you can't play hockey. You are going to struggle now that you can't perform physically. You will be thinking about what's next in your life now that you will not feel fulfilled through scoring goals. Anytime, there are life altering situations like changing jobs, injury, losing a family member, getting traded or simply changing careers, we challenge our identity and purpose, and we feel anxious and insecure. That insecurity feels like a red alert or a 911 emergency."

Elliott said "Yup, I have some of all that for sure."

Ranger replied. "You see, now you can't perform for God in the hockey arena with goals and assists or evaluate yourself based upon your time on ice. Today is no different than before your accident in one especially important way. God loved you before your accident, after your accident, and He loved you yesterday, and today and He will love you tomorrow. When God is your source, you can do all new things thru Christ! He will be the one who strengthens you.

"Elliott today you get the opportunity to step out on faith and not on your ability to perform. Today you get to ask God how you will glorify Him with your passions and abilities. You see, it's not about what you chase, for today you will discover that what belongs to you will find you. Your purpose has never changed. Your purpose is to glorify Him with your talents and abilities. Elliott, in the coming days and weeks, maybe months, you will amplify your purpose with vision. You will find a strategy to execute your vision, and find a communication platform for your brand's vision, and we will pray about the seven steps together. Elliott, I am so thankful for you and the vision that is inside of you. Together we will take action, together we will win.

"I have to go, but I will leave you with this. If you want to go fast, then go alone. If you want to go far, go together. Elliott, we are going to go far together, because you are not alone! All right, we will chat more. I have to go."

"Thank you, Ranger. I wasn't expecting that! Thank you." Elliott said.

"Ok, you got it". Ranger replied and hung up.

Elliott was inspired and encouraged for the first time in a long while. He had hope, though he didn't understand yet, exactly why.

KELLY AT ST. CLOUD

After the injury, Kelly supported Elliott mentally, emotionally, physically and spiritually. She was with Elliott almost every day. She loved Elliott and nothing was going to separate them, but Kelly knew she had to live her life too. After three months of going from the hospital to Elliott's house, to sleeping in the hospital, she was exhausted. Kelly's and Elliott's moms both approached her and said "We are thankful for all the time and energy you have given to Elliott. Thank you for everything you have done, but you have a life of your own and we want to honor you in what you have done with your academic and athletic career. We think you should focus more on playing hockey and getting good grades."

School was about to start, and Kelly agreed she needed to get back on the ice. Elliott confirmed that he appreciated her, but he also encouraged her to focus on her own priorities. Though it was a bit over the top, Elliott said, "Kelly, I am crippled, but I am not dead. I am here, so let's look at what life has for each of us in the future."

Kelly was relieved, and if she was honest with herself, she was looking forward to learning more about sports psychology and the study of human behavior.

Kelly stepped into her first psychology class at Saint Cloud State University and it was crystal clear that this was the course of study she was meant to pursue. After sitting in class and hearing the professor talk about behavior and purpose, passion, vision, and mission and values, she felt at home. That evening, she reflected on her conversations with JJ and her time at FCA Hockey camp and wrote this in her journal:

PURPOSE– *is the reason something is created. What is our human purpose? In my personal worldview, God created us in His image so that we can glorify Him with our passions, talents, and abilities. These passions, talents, and abilities can be and should be communicated via our vision, mission and core values. A person without purpose is lost. A* *person without a passion has no vision, mission or core values. A person without purpose has doubt, anxiety and stress, poor self-image and a whole host of other issues.*

PASSIONS– *are something you love to do and would do for free. These passions may include being a transformer, teacher, builder, creator, conceiver, processor, connector, altruist, or healer.*

DESTINY- *short for destination. In my worldview the journey is the destination. God moving in our life every day is the destination. Glorifying him in everything we do is the destination.*

VISION *is a clearly written image of the future. Vision is the North Star; something you aim for, but never accomplish. Vision uses the Limbic system. The Limbic system processes emotion. Vision is a short, portable, easy to understand, memorable and inspiring statement. The statement itself should go outside my personal effort. The vision should amplify the purpose. Vision answers the "why" question.*

MISSION– the steps to the vision. If Vision would be the top of the roof, then the mission statements are the supporting beams that would hold the roof up. Mission statements engage the neocortex of the brain, vision is the limbic. Mission statements answer the who, what, where, when, and how conversations.

CORE VALUES– *Are day to day guiding principles*

or philosophies. Examples include Hard work, integrity, honesty, character, respect, responsibility, and servant leadership.

Kelly didn't know what to do with these notes, but it was exactly what she had been seeking for a very long time. She didn't know why, but she reflected on these thoughts when she gave her life to the Lord back at the FCA Hockey Camp and in her time with JJ. It was all coming together, and she had a feeling of preparedness and completeness coming over her. She felt mentally strong.

THAT NIGHT

After talking with Elliott, Kelly was powering down, reflecting on the day, and she was thinking about her school notes. Although she was very tempted to get them out and reread them, she realized she left her book bag downstairs. The house was cold, so she was tucked in bed in her favorite jammies. She couldn't sleep, and she didn't want to get out of bed. She didn't know what to do, but her mind was racing. There was so much change going on with Elliott's accident and JJ's death. Kelly had been going back and forth from St Cloud to Edina, which was about an hour drive. When Kelly talked to Elliott, like she had moments earlier, he was depressed and most of the time he was distant and rarely happy. Elliott's life had turned upside down and Kelly's seemed to be on autopilot. No, she didn't like the feeling. She had lost her motivation to play hockey, and she wanted to be with Elliott. Selfishly she wanted to play hockey and learn how to be a sports psychologist. It was getting late and her eyes started to get heavy. She fell asleep thinking, *What is the future I am fighting for?*

NOW WHAT?

Everyone around Elliott was adjusting to the new normal. Kelly was going to school, playing hockey and traveling back and forth to be with Elliott as much as she could. Elliott was tired most of the time. He was trying to manage the wheelchair, rehab, phone calls, and his snail mail. People from all over the world sent him letters and Elliott enjoyed reading them. It gave him a sense of confidence. These days he really didn't know his purpose or vision, but he knew there was something for him. For now, he was going through the motions of life trying to establish a new normal. He reflected on JJ, his time at FCA Hockey and his passion to do something great. He just didn't know why or how to put it together. He had no path.

CHAPTER NINE

A NEW VISION

Several months after the injury, a package arrived in the mail from "The Estate of Jeremiah James." Elliott was confined to a wheelchair but could use his hands, so he opened each letter and box himself, which was a good thing. He had been getting more mail from around the world since ESPN did a special on him. When he got home from the hospital, his folks moved his bed into the old playroom, which was bigger and easier for Elliott to move around in with the wheelchair.

Elliott opened the package and inside was a letter that read:

Our dad talked about you and Kelly often. My brother and I wanted you to have his original copy. Signed JJ's Kids. David and William.

Elliott immediately broke down in tears as he looked at the book. It was really well done, but very old. You could tell someone had flipped through the pages dozens of times.

The only thing written on the front cover was R7.

Elliott flipped to the opening page where all it said was, "Vision Wins!"

Elliott turned another few pages and saw a list of steps.

Step 1: Destiny
Step 2: Vision
Step 3: Strategy
Step 4: Brand
Step 5: Communicate
Step 6: Pray
Step 7: Action

As he wiped his tears, he remembered JJ's life and a feeling of inspiration came over him. All of a sudden, he was hyper-focused. He hadn't had that feeling in a very long time. He was inspired by direction and felt interested in life again. A lot of people were feeling sorry for him and supporting him, and he was thankful, but deep down he wanted to be valued, appreciated, and loved because of his contribution to the world, not because he was injured. His identity as a hockey player had been violated and stripped away. He had been completely removed from the hockey community into something totally unfamiliar. He had always been around the rink, working out, talking hockey, and now he was confined to his room in a wheelchair. Life had taken a very unexpected turn and he was frustrated, distant and withdrawn. He was basically angry all the time, but this was not consistent with his desired attitude and outlook on life. He felt like he had been standing on a corner in a city

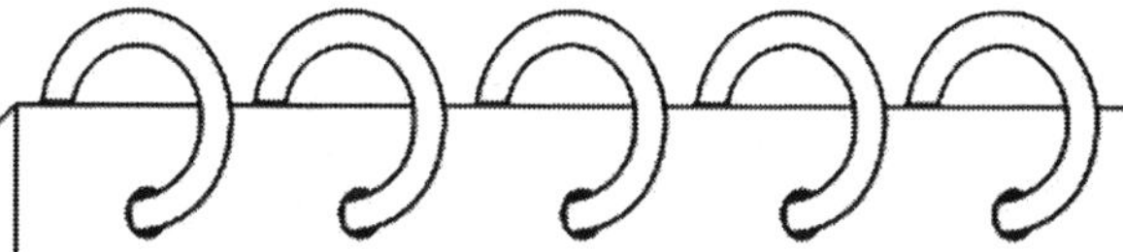

R7 Steps:

Step 1: Destiny
Step 2: Vision
Step 3: Strategy
Step 4: Brand
Step 5: Communicate
Step 6: Pray
Step 7: Action

he had never been in. His mind, body, and spirit were completely lost, with no hope in sight.

FLASHBACK

Elliott's mind flashed back to moments he shared with JJ. He flipped through the journal and he stopped on Step 2, where the top of the page read, "Vision Wins- what is the future you are fighting for?" On the very next page, Elliott saw a list of personal vision statements and two immediately stood out to him:

Every day, I am obsessed with helping people become better. Bambi

Impacting the world of hockey through Jesus, one coach and one player at time. Ranger

Elliott immediately shouted, "Mom!"

Mary and Steve came rushing up the stairs to the room where Elliott was sitting. They rushed in and Mary said, "Honey are you ok? What is going on, buddy?"

Elliott replied. "Mom, can you call Kelly? I need to talk to her right now. Mom, I need to talk to Kelly. Please call her for me?"

Mary called Kelly and within minutes Elliott was on the phone with her.

"Kelly, you're not going to believe what just happened. Do you remember JJ's last words to us?"

"Umm, let me think," Kelly replied. But before she could answer, Elliott said, "Kelly, I have JJ's blueprint. I have his master plan to becoming the best version of myself! There is so much clarity here! I remember him saying to us the day before he died that he would give us all the info we needed. Remember that, Kelly? I think this is what he was talking about. Kelly, I have the path."

Elliott didn't know why he said this but then he said, "Thank you Jesus! I am alive."

"Kelly, I want to talk to you more than ever about our encounters with JJ. I need to go back in time and understand his words to you and me. Will you help me?"

Kelly was happy that Elliott was excited over something, as the past year had been stressful, awkward and disappointing., She was eager and excited to help him. Kelly responded, "Absolutely! Elliott, when do you want me to come over?"

Elliott said, "Anytime. I know you are busy with school and hockey but anytime, anytime. Thank you, Kelly, I love you!"

"I love you too, Elliott," said Kelly.

For the next several weeks and months, Kelly and Elliott went through JJ's journal and tried to go back in time and rethink their brief, but frequent conversations with him.

THE MAN THAT GOD CALLED HIM TO BECOME

One late night, after going through the journal step by step and word for word for several weeks, Elliott looked at Kelly and said, "You know, Kelly, we have been through this over and over again and I keep going back to living a life of fulfillment through people, power and possessions. I realize now that the plan JJ and even Ranger was talking about was not having a vision through achievement, people, power, and possessions, but having fulfillment through a vision that served a higher power, or a higher purpose, like through God or Jesus. Through my injury, which I now want to refer to as my opportunity, I have been awakened to my real purpose in life. I know this sounds strange but these past weeks, I feel more alive than I have ever felt before. I feel like I have the opportunity to live a life of significance, and that I don't have to achieve at hockey to be fulfilled, but I can live a life of empowerment and empathy. It's weird, but for the first time in my life I feel like my identity is not in my time on ice, or goals and assists.

Kelly, my identity is not in what I do, but who I am and how I love. It's how I express love for myself and others."

This all sounded weird for Elliott to say, but it was what he was feeling, and it felt right to say it now because he wanted to find the right path to express his vision and love for others.

Over the next several months, Elliott began to pray and meditate about the vision he felt God had given him. He thought about Bambi and how she made an impact on children, and how Ranger made an impact on youth hockey players, and how JJ made an impact on the youth. He thought, *I want to make an impact on the youth and our next generation, but he also had the thought that he might be too young to think that way.*

Back in high school, he read what Abraham Lincoln had done for slaves and thought maybe there was something he could do about human trafficking, since that was the issue that devastated Bambi's family. He knew the idea of getting involved in something like this would stretch him mentally, emotionally, physically, and spiritually. He knew if he went in this direction it would test his faith muscle, and he knew he had no faith muscle. He reflected on Bambi's story and how she was filled with joy, peace, patience and self-control. He knew he needed to borrow some of her faith, because he didn't have any and didn't know what it meant to trust God. But he did know how Bambi's American mom and dad stepped up in faith. Elliott had studied JJ's process, and he did not take any shortcuts, highlighting every word in his journal. He knew that the vision had to be easy to understand. It had to be short, seven to eleven words with no conjunctions or prepositional phrases. The emphasis of the vision had to be inspiring.

The more he thought and prayed about it, the more he sensed God was saying to his heart that he should commit his life to spreading the message about the evil world of human trafficking, sex trafficking, and the exploitation of children and labor. He had learned that these heinous industries had been referred to by industry experts as the new era of "Modern-Day Slavery." He wanted to bring light to this dark world, in much the same way as Ranger was bringing the light of Christ to the youth hockey world.

Elliott had written several variations of a vision around all kinds of abuse, but he loved this simple version, which he wrote on the front page of JJ's journal:

Vision: To End All Forms of Modern-Day Slavery.

The next day, Elliott and Kelly started to reorganize JJ's journal. It wasn't that the journal was confusing, but Elliott and Kelly wanted to really absorb the information. They thought it would help to write it out as they saw it.

> R7 for Organizations
> Step 1: Destiny
> Step 2: Vision
> Step 3: Strategy
> Step 4: Brand
> Step 5: Communicate
> Step 6: Pray
> Step 7: Action

Kelly and Elliott wrote their list on one sheet of paper and began to study it. Kelly said, "Wow! That is a lot of information. No wonder JJ didn't blast it at us. Can you imagine if he tried to share all this in one

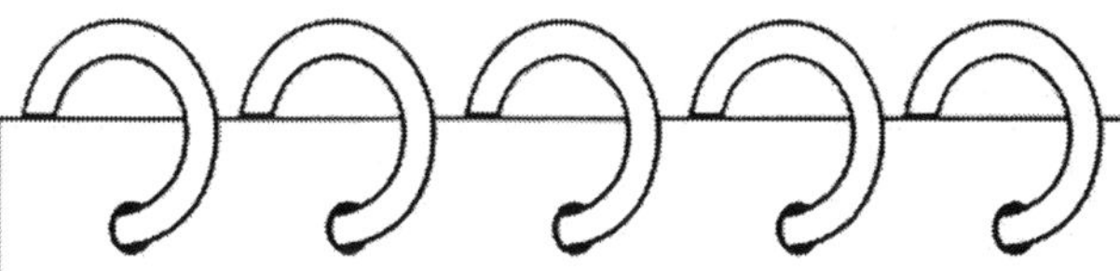

R7 for Organizations:

Step 1: Destiny

Step 2: Vision

Step 3: Strategy

Step 4: Brand

Step 5: Communicate

Step 6: Pray

Step 7: Action

sitting? JJ had a lot of information in his brain, and he knew the best way to share it with us was one idea at a time."

Elliott replied, "I think it was more than information; it was wisdom!"

With all this in mind, Elliott knew immediately what he wanted to do. It was like he saw the puck in the corner and was going to be the first one there. He didn't waste any time. "Kelly," he said, "Let's apply rigor to Vision. Let's follow these steps and build our R7 plan to help God's children. I mean, after all, Bambi is doing it through power skating and Ranger is doing it with FCA hockey. Why can't we do it too?"

Elliott paused and just looked at her, not giving her a chance to answer his question.

"Kelly," Elliott said, "I love you, and am so thankful for you." It was the first time since his accident that he felt valued, appreciated, and loved. He was finally able to reach out to Kelly and express his true feelings. He had an overwhelming feeling of joy.

Kelly hugged Elliott and replied, "Ok," my hero, "let's get to work! We have a new vision: To End Modern-Day Slavery. What do we do next?"

"Well, let's see," said Elliott. "We probably need to go to step three and write up our power thoughts. Before we do though, let's use JJ's checklist to make sure our vision fits. I love it, and I am inspired by it, but let's make sure we get it right."

Kelly had the best handwriting in the world. It was neat, clean, and sexy. He couldn't explain sexy handwriting, but Kelly had it. Plus, he had limited use with his hands, so she could write way better than he could now. Even though the doctors told Elliott he may never have functional use of his hands and arms again, he didn't listen to them. Nothing was impossible for His God. But for now, Kelly would be his hands and do the writing!

Kelly wrote:
The Vision Checklist is:

1) Simple
2) Easy to understand
3) Portable
4) Inspiring
5) Empowering
6) Detailed
7) People Oriented
8) Memorable
9) have the God factor (go outside your personal effort).

"Kelly," said Elliott, "I'm confused about what you mean by "Portable."

Kelly explained, I think it means we can take it with us. Elliott stopped her and said, "I remember when I read JJ's notes on this. He had an example and scripture reference for it. His notes said something

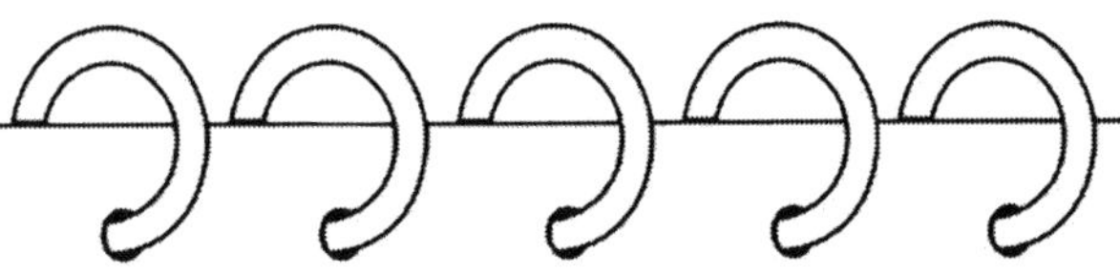

The Vision Checklist:

1) Simple

2) Easy to Understand

3) Portable

4) Inspiring

5) Empowering

6) Detailed

7) People Oriented

8) Memorable

9) Have the God Factor

(go outside your personal effort)

like, "When you drive by a billboard on the freeway and it says, 'McDonalds, next exit.' I can remember these three words as I drive one mile down the road, and I can remember to turn off at the exit."

Kelly interrupted him and said, "Ok, yeah ok the words are portable I can take them with me. I remember there being a scripture reference next to the word billboard."

Kelly went back and looked at JJ original notes. "Here it is," she explained. "It says Habakkuk 2:2." Kelly and Elliott didn't know what it meant so Kelly did a quick google search on her phone, and she read this to Elliott ``Then the Lord replied: write down the revelation and make it plain on the tablets so that a herald may run with it." They both looked at each other, sort of confused and Elliott said, "Ok, let's unpack this!"

Kelly read. "Then the Lord replied." Elliott interrupted her and said, "Ok so the Lord is talking to this dude, not a big deal." Elliott smirked and Kelly laughed.

"Ok," Kelly said, "Write the revelation down."
Elliott thought for a second and said, "Our revelation is our vision...got it."

Kelly said, "Right!"

Kelly read it again. "Make it plain on a tablet."

Elliott replied, "I bet it means in your nice handwriting, so someone else could read it and put it on a plain tablet where there were no other words or graphics."

Kelly said, "Yeah, I remember in one of my PowerPoint classes, Mrs. Smith said that I had too many pictures and too much text on one PowerPoint slide and that I needed to put less information on the one slide and create two or three slides for the idea."

Elliott said, "Exactly, keep the message clean and simple."

Kelly jumped in and kept reading, "that a herald may run with it."

Elliott said, "I get it. If there's too much information, a herald may not be able to run with it. Kind of like your PowerPoint example, if there is too much information on one slide then the reader gets confused and doesn't understand the point you are trying to make. All the information might be good, but the reader gets bogged down and can't process the information."

Kelly was confused. "Ok, last question! What is a herald?"

Elliott replied, "I don't know."

Kelly did another google search. She read the results to Elliott, "an official messenger bringing news." They both looked at each other. Kelly said, "Elliott are you an official messenger?"

A NEW VISION

They each had shivers run down their spine. They had the feeling of inspiration as if they scored their first goal. They knew something special had just happened.

Both Kelly and Elliott went down the checklist and said "yes" to everything. The last question tripped them up a little bit. Elliott said aloud, "Does it have the God factor (go outside your personal effort)?" Elliott looked at Kelly and said, "What do you think this means?"

Kelly replied thoughtfully. "You are a hockey player, and you know nothing about sex slavery, forced labor, or this whole Modern-Day Slavery thing! You need God! With you alone, it's impossible, but with God all things are possible, Elliott."

Elliott didn't know what just happened, but they were both surprised at what Kelly said.

They laughed and agreed that God was going to be the center of all their plans. Check that off the list. There is no doubt that God would want us to end all Modern-Day Slavery. That's a God factor if there ever was one!

Kelly and Elliott felt comfortable with their vision "To End Modern-Day Slavery."

"What now?" Elliott said as he turned to look at Kelly. "Let's look at Step three."

They looked down at the sheet of paper and they both said, "Strategy."

Elliott started talking while he was thinking. Kelly liked that he was inspired and encouraged, so she let him talk and think at the same time.

Elliott said, "You know when I was preparing for the game, I would do this Here and Now exercise during the National Anthem. It allowed me to clear my mind from past events and let go of any anxiety and stress about future events or situations. I would go through my routine going around my face. What did I see, hear, smell, taste and feel? My first year of Juniors, I started to incorporate Empathy and High and Low EI into my routine. I don't know if this is right, but what if I take those same lessons and apply them to the End Modern-Day Slavery vision?"

Kelly said, "That's brilliant. Let's try it."

So, right there in Elliott's room, both Elliott and Kelly closed their eyes and started to go through their mental preparation pregame routine but apply it to what they needed to do to end Modern-Day Slavery.

For the next few minutes as Kelly went through the routine, it was absolutely quiet; nothing was moving, but their thoughts. They were both experts in the mental preparation process but had no idea what they could do about ending Modern-Day Slavery!

Kelly spoke first, "Here is a list of things I think we are going to need. She just rattled them off:

Prayer
Time
Patience
Friends that are wiser than we are

Elliott expanded the list with:

Money
Problem
Solution
An awesome Team
Prayer
A Plan... a really good plan"

They both opened their eyes and looked at each other and said, "What did you say?" They both laughed. Elliott and Kelly were confused by both their responses, so Kelly reached for another piece of paper and wrote down all their thoughts as they began to prioritize their lists. After some back and forth discussions, this was their revised list:

1. A really good plan
2. Figure out the problem and solution
3. Find a killer team-people that are wiser than us
4. Money
5. Prayer
6. Patience

After looking at the list again, they scratched "a really good plan" and switched Prayer and Money. They didn't know why they did that; it just felt right to both of them. Here was their final strategy.

1. Figure out the problem and solution
2. Find a killer team-people that are wiser than us
3. Prayer
4. Money
5. Patience

ESPN

Over the next couple of weeks, Elliott began to make a list of "Killer" friends that could help them "End Modern-Day Slavery." They hadn't communicated their list to anyone, as they were creating their strategy together. They were trying to figure out the problem/solution formula to end Modern-Day slavery.

Elliott was thinking back on what made him a successful hockey player, and he realized he watched a lot of videos. Over the years, he did a lot of research on NHL players: their habits, tendencies, workout schedules, and nutritional suggestions. Elliott loved research, so while Kelly was at school, he read everything he could find, and listened to Ted Talks and Podcasts on Modern-Day Slavery. He researched the different non-profit organizations and NGOs that were trying to attack the problem of Modern-Day Slavery. He researched labor costs and products that were associated with slave labor and the profit associated with it. He researched where children were being enslaved, and how they were being enslaved and how they were being used for sex or forced labor.

A NEW VISION

Elliott looked at what countries and what companies were supporting and not supporting Modern-Day slavery efforts. Elliott was passionate about finding as much information as possible. He researched forced marriage, child slavery, human trafficking, domestic slavery and the products of slavery. He thoroughly educated himself on all forms of Modern-Day Slavery. He was at it day and night. He found something called the "Global Slavery Index" and summarized the following stats:

- 45.8 million people are involved in Modern-Day Slavery around the world
- 150 billion dollars contribute to global profits each year because of this enslavement
- Modern-Day Slavery is the second largest international crime behind illicit drugs
- The type of slavery includes:
  1. Bonded Labor or debt bondage
  2. Forced Labor: 90% of these people are exploited by individuals or enterprises
- 21 million people are in forced labor
- 5.5 million children are involved in child slavery including:
  1. Physical labor and domestic slavery
  2. Fighters in armed conflict
  3. Commercial sexual abuse

Elliott had a good working definition of human trafficking. He wrote it down in his notes. Human trafficking is the act of recuring or transferring a person by the means of coercion, abduction, or deception for the purpose of exploitation. After looking at his numbers and doing months of research, he concluded that forced labor was more profitable and more widely used by individuals and companies to create a profit than was child slavery. When he did a simple Google search, he found child slavery to be more prevalent than forced labor. He quickly realized there was a problem with how this market was being perceived. It seemed clear that everyone acknowledged a child slavery problem, when in fact, there was a forced labor problem. All the images in Google had child slavery images, but there was a branding problem and Elliott thought he could fix it.

CHAPTER TEN

THE STRATEGY

Kelly and Elliott came up with a long list of problems and solutions, but they realized there was really only one real problem and one real solution, Remembering the R7 principles, they decided to go with one simple idea. Kelly wrote this idea on another piece of paper.

Problem: Modern-Day Slavery includes human trafficking, sex trafficking, and the exploitation of child labor.

Solution: End Modern-Day Slavery by creating awareness. Do this by talking to as many people as possible and ask them to give their time, resources, and money to bring about change.

Elliott was convinced that to make a difference, he needed to become the best-informed person on all matters related to Modern-Day Slavery. It was his vision and his purpose. Kelly continually encouraged him to review his notes to be sure everything was according to what JJ taught them about building a strong R7 foundation.

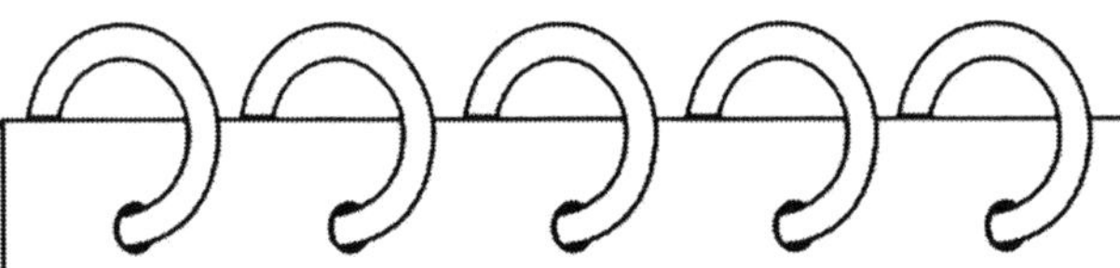

Our Strategy:

- Figure out the problem & solution

- Find a killer team - people that are wiser than us

- Prayer

- Money

- Patience

THE STRATEGY

Elliott reviewed JJ's notes. There were check marks next to Step 1: Destiny. Step 2: Vision. Step 3: Strategy. He felt really good that so far, he had managed to follow JJ's R7 process. He was ready to tackle the next steps and was anxious to put check marks next to Step 4 and Step 5.

Elliott was sitting at his adaptive work desk and JJ's journal was across the room, so he asked Kelly, "What are steps 4 and 5?"

Kelly said, "Step 4 is Brand and Step 5 is Communicate."

Elliott said, "This is so good. I am super excited. We are on track Kelly! Just out of curiosity, what are steps 6 and 7?"

Kelly checked the journal again and said, "Step 6 is Pray and Step 7 is Action."

Elliott was focused now and said, "Ok, that is perfect. Kelly, I have several media interviews coming up. One is with ESPN. I want to get T-shirts made that say, "It's not a fair fight."

Kelly thought about that and said, "What about steps 4 and 5? Are we jumping to step 7 and taking action?"

"Kelly," Elliott said, "I am going back to Step three, Strategy." Kelly was really confused.

Elliott replied, "This is a process, not a program. We have to use what God is giving us right now. This is not my plan, or your plan. This is His plan. I worked on my plan and look at what it got me!"

The disappointment in his voice was clear, as he said softly, "I am stuck in a wheelchair for the rest of my life."

Elliott continued, "I want to do God's plan. This has to be what JJ was talking about when he first started sharing all this with us. I get it now. We need to do God's plan because we are on God's timeline, not ours. Let's follow JJ's process, but be sensitive to what God is giving us. Right now, He has given us a platform. We are going to use this platform to help God's people that are being used and manipulated for the purpose of financial exploitation. This is how we are going to End Modern-Day Slavery. Kelly, we have a vision and it's really good. In fact, it's awesome. Our next step is to find a killer team.

"Remember our strategy. We need to go back to Step 3: Strategy. Our second item on our list was to find a killer team. Kelly interrupted him and said, "Elliott, you are right. Let's communicate the vision early and often and then go find a killer team.

Kelly was blown away at Elliott's critical thinking skills and data processing abilities. She went on to explain that winning is hard and having great people around you who have talent and are wise makes winning less difficult. She said, "Teams I have been on over the years had lots of talent, but when you don't play well together, it's frustrating and no fun."

"Come to think of it," Kelly continued, "All my high school teams were super talented, but the coach would have to constantly yell at us and say, "if we don't work together for a common goal, we will not win."

He would later show us videos of other teams with talent who didn't win. In fact, they lost most of the time, especially the teams that had one or two really good players, who tried to do it all themselves.

"Exactly," Elliott said.

Kelly added, "If you want to go fast, you go alone," and Elliott finished her statement with, "and if you want to go far, you go together."

Kelly replied. "Let's Go!"

Elliott said, "Listen, I have a tremendous platform right now. Everyone wants to talk to me. My Twitter and Instagram pages are continually lighting up.

"For the next several weeks, I am going to find a killer team. I am going to communicate my new vision to end Modern-Day Slavery to anyone and everyone who will give me time on their platform. I am going to talk early and often to everyone who will listen. Everyone keeps asking me, "You are only 21, what does life look like next?" I am going to tell them. "We need to help God's children by putting a spotlight on the evil and satanic methods and practices of all Modern-Day Slavery including human trafficking, sex trafficking, and the exploitation of child labor.

With God's help, we are going to end Modern-Day Slavery. I am going to take all the lessons I learned from hockey and apply them to my revised vision."

Elliott was cataloging some of the lessons he learned from his hockey days. He was thinking to himself, I am going to mentally, emotionally, physically, and spiritually, come early, and stay late. I am going to do my here and now exercises for meetings and interviews prior to the meetings and interviews, I am going to work on my main points before I show up, sort of like my ABC's that I learned through hockey mental preparation. I am going to be a master of my emotions, I will not be Low EI or slave to my emotions when talking to people that don't understand my points, vision, or mission. I can't let negative self-talk dominate my thinking. I need to stay positive, and I need to stay in the power channel.

And then he said with a louder voice like he was communicating on stage to a thousand people, "I am going to communicate that it's an unfair fight, show them the stats that I have accumulated and express my opinion on what we are up against with the facts about Modern-Day Slavery. I will ask them to join my team so that we can create awareness and get them involved in actively giving, praying or serving. There will be lots of ways to get involved," Elliott exclaimed.

Kelly looked at him and was so impressed with how he was coming alive. She had goose bumps running down her back and arms. She could see how Elliott was being filled with God's power and how JJ had laid the foundation for a winning formula. She thought to herself: *I wonder why JJ chose us and I wonder if JJ was praying for us back then.* Then she corrected herself and thought, *wait a second, JJ didn't pick us. God picked us... JJ saw God in us!*

If she had a mic she would have dropped it and left the room.

Kelly loved that Elliott was fired up with a new passion and commitment like she had never seen before. At the same time, she had restless nights because she knew she could not be as engaged as Elliott was with his vision to end Modern-Day Slavery. She wanted that same passion and commitment for her own vision. After going through this process with Elliott, she knew she still wanted to be the best teammate on the planet. She could support Elliott in every way possible, but she wanted to find that same level of passion and commitment for herself. Right now, she had a fire to pursue about becoming a sports psychologist. She had learned that her identity was not about playing hockey. She was looking to the future of how she could be the best teammate on the planet with the sports psychology lens. She took all of JJ's words and written processes to heart. She would support Elliott and many other athletes and professionals who struggled with performance and identity. Just like a seed had been planted inside Elliott, a similar kind of seed was growing inside her heart and mind.

THE POWER OF WHO

"Ranger here," said Ranger.

"This is Elliott," said a light-hearted voice.

Ranger continued, "Hey what's going on Elliott? How are you holding up and how can I help you?"

Elliott was excited that Ranger was interested in helping him and said, "Well Ranger, I want to thank you for all your prayers and for reaching out to me and my family over this last year."

Ranger replied, "Excuse me, just hold on one second."

Elliott could hear Ranger giving someone instructions in the background and then he heard," Ok, Ok, got it."

Ranger's voice was loud now, so Elliott could tell he was back talking to him.

Ranger apologized for the interruption and went on to say, "No problem, glad we could help. Is there any particular way that we can help now?"

"Well Ranger," Elliott said, with new enthusiasm in his voice. "I need your help in a new way. I don't know what I am doing, but according to JJ and his R7 process, I need to communicate my vision early and often with those who might get it. I know you have done this yourself with great success. You have an amazing team of Godly warriors around the country, maybe even around the world, and I want to see if you can help me build awareness around this new vision God has given me."

Ranger said, "Sure I would love to help. Tell me about your new vision God has given you. What do you need from me? I would love to help you, Elliott."

"Well, here is what I am planning to do for the next several months. I am going to find a killer team. Will you help me build an amazing team of Men and Women of God to help me communicate this vision?

Ranger said, "Keep going."

Elliott was on a roll! "From sun-up to sun-down, I'm going to build awareness of the evil of Modern-Day Slavery. I am trusting JJ's process, but I am also disgusted by this thing that is happening all over the world and right here at home! Everyone keeps asking me what life looks like next, and I am going to tell them that I'm going to take all the tools I learned in preparing to play hockey and apply what I have learned to upgrade my journey and bring new opportunity. So I am stepping out on faith and I immediately thought of you since you know a thing or two about vision, faith and helping God's children.

Ranger chuckled and said, "Yeah!" and laughed some more.

Elliott continued, "I am going all in on this and asking God to direct my every thought, word and step.

I want to be a catalyst to expose this evil and end this new era of Modern-Day Slavery. I am going to communicate that it's an unfair fight, show everyone who will listen to me about the stats I have accumulated and voice my opinion on what we are up against. I will ask them to join me or us in this battle.

"Honestly, Ranger, I am asking if you are willing to help me and my team, our team, so that we can create greater awareness and get people involved in acting, giving, praying or serving?
Ranger, will you help me?"

Ranger hesitated for several seconds. He was reflecting on everything he had going on. He said a quick prayer for guidance and instantly felt the Lord's presence. He felt the right thing to do was to say, yes, but he had no idea how he was going to fit this into his schedule. He knew God would direct each step, so he prayed again and whispered to himself, "Your will be done, Lord. Not mine, Your will be done."

To Elliott the quiet time felt like an eternity. Finally, Ranger said, "Yes, whatever you need from me, I will help you Elliott. We will help you with the vision God has given you and help you to spread the word to help end Modern-Day Slavery. You let me know where and when and I will be there."

Elliott was elated. He said, "Thank you Ranger, you have changed my life, yet again"

Elliott hung up the phone and said his own prayer. "Thank You, Lord, for Ranger's help, and Yours! I believe I can do all things through You, the One who strengthen me."

In the coming weeks and months, Ranger and Elliott worked closely together, going through Ranger's list of powerful men and women of God. That list extended into ESPN Executives, current and former NHL players. It turned out that those executives and current and former NHL players had lists of their own that extended to other executives, movie producers, and 1% income earners in the world. They reached out to airline executives, hospitality, and food and beverage executives, and within three months, Elliott had an email distribution and social network list of power influencers of over five million people. Word travels fast when God is behind it!

SIX MONTHS LATER

Elliott officially started his foundation when he had raised over twenty million dollars. He built a killer team comprised of some of the wealthiest Christian business owners in the country, including labor force officials, veterans, and doctors from the most respected hospitals around the world. His foundation had board members and scouts who each reported back to Elliott with stories for their online community to learn, give and act. Their nonprofit foundation signed petitions, created awareness, and got people involved, and they did it really well. Over twenty million actions were taken, 5.6 million Facebook fans were generated, 195 countries joined in to be part of their vision, and 113 global partners acted as watchdogs concerning forced and sex slavery.

After many interviews and fundraising banquets and webinars, Ranger decided it was time to engage in step seven: "Take Action" from JJ's R7 process. They needed to engage in more prayer and more action.

Step 6 meant they had to put together a prayer team. The prayer team actively prayed for the foundation and for Elliott. They prayed about steps one through five which included, his purpose, the vision, the strategy, the brand, the communication and the action plan. They prayed for a well-executed and efficient purpose, vision, strategy, and brand. They prayed to communicate their vision to end Modern-Day slavery with boldness and build their brand moving forward. Simply put, Modern-Day Slavery is evil and they knew they needed to expose it. Elliott knew there were issues with the global image, but he also knew he had a great process with R7. He trusted that steps one through six were solid, so now it was time to further engage step seven...to act.

Although her time was limited, Kelly continued to study Sports Psychology at SCS and support and encourage Elliott. She knew her purpose was to glorify God with her talents and abilities through sports and sensed her own vision of becoming the best teammate on the planet. God was exposing this vision to her almost daily. She was extremely excited for Elliott. She knew she was in the learning stages of her career. She had mapped out a seven year plan to get her Doctorate in Sports and Performance Psychology. She didn't know how it was going to come together but she was really inspired to be the best teammate and serve her team and Elliott through patience, peace, self-control and understanding. She wanted to learn more about mental toughness and coping strategies to serve athletes and love Elliott. She was encouraged by Elliott and she knew she had a way to go in her personal development. She wanted to be there for Elliott as he communicated and executed his new vision.

CHAPTER ELEVEN

THE SPEECH

Through Ranger, Bambi's connections, lots of emails, and phone calls, Elliott found himself at the side of the stage at the General Assembly of the United Nations Global Convention for the Suppression of Human Trafficking in New York City.

While he was waiting at the edge of the stage, he glanced at his watch and noticed it was December second. Elliott was whispering to himself and mentally going through his notes. He was thinking and whispering that we all have a role to play before we bring an end, once and for all to Modern-Day Slavery. He was thinking that today is an epic day for exposing the evils of human trafficking, sex trafficking, and the exploitation of child labor. He thought, I can do all things through Christ who strengthens me. This day, December second will be a significant day for everyone in this room. He prayed and asked God to save lives and change hearts today. His physiology was changing because his heart rate was increasing, and he was getting more excited about what God was doing through him and his talks.

As Elliott mentally rehearsed his notes, he gained

confidence with every thought. He had JJ's R7 process nailed down, and Ranger, and Bambi's mentorship behind him. Today, by God's grace and mercy, he was going to be a difference maker. He was going to win. His notes were in his lap as he anxiously wheeled himself out to the front of the stage. As he looked down at his notes one last time, he saw his handwritten note that said: Step 1- Purpose: glorify Him. He said to himself, *My purpose today is to glorify God who has blessed me with my talents and abilities. I will do this by communicating the vision He gave me. He looked up and said to himself: Vision wins when I work the Vision. R7 ...Let's go!*

He heard his introduction, just as he whispered the words "R7 ... let's go!"

"Our keynote speaker this year is a man that knows more about tragedy and success than perhaps most any other person in this room. Elliott Podofski was a perennial hockey player. At the age of 15 and again at 17, he was Minnesota High School Hockey State Champion for the Edina Hornets. He was committed to a full athletic scholarship at Saint Cloud State in Saint Cloud Minnesota. At the age of 18, he was drafted in the first round by the Carolina Hurricanes. For two years, he played in Juniors with the Fargo Force in the USHL. At age 21, just 14 seconds into his first collegiate hockey game, he accidently fell into the boards headfirst and cracked his 4th and 5th vertebrae. Today, Elliott is here to share his story and his journey with us. In his success with hockey, Elliott reminds us that though one dream has died, another vision has successfully emerged. I am so honored to welcome Elliott Podofski to the stage today."

"Let's give a warm welcome to Elliott Podofski!"

Elliott wheeled himself out to the front of the stage and got himself situated, adjusting the mic.

The crowd patiently waited

He looked up and saw over 2,500 people. Way in the back, he could see rows of broadcast cameras, each blinking red, which meant it was game on. The world was watching and waiting to hear Elliott's story and vision.

Before Elliott began his speech, he took another look at the crowd and tried to absorb the moment as he glanced across the room, his heart was moved with inspiration as he saw Bambi, Kelly, Ranger, Ranger's wife, and his parents sitting in the front row and waiting with bated breath. He knew they were each praying for him. He could feel God's presence and he relaxed.

Elliott began, *I am a 22-year-old stepping out in faith. Before my accident, I was spiritually dead and now with limited use of my arms and legs, I am spiritually alive! How does that happen?*

One word: God! That's how that happens.

I am alive and my purpose is to serve Him, and that is why I am here. Today I am here for God's children.

Today I am here to put the biggest spotlight I can on the evil world of Modern-Day Slavey.

You see my injury sparked a discovery process. I have learned that a dream is an idea that sparks a vision. A vision is more than a dream; it's actually lots of little dreams backed by the purpose and passions in your life. Today, I stand before you, that is, I sit before you, with a new vision. Elliott flashed a big grin, and the crowd laughed a nervous laugh. As I sit before you today, I am reminded that we all have dreams inside of us. In recent months, I have had time to think about and process my dream of playing in the NHL and what has changed in my life since my injury. Through my tragedy I have had to pivot on my purpose in life. In fact, I have had to take on the challenge of my will vs. God's will in my life, and of course, God won. It wasn't an easy fight. Through lots of surrendering, mentorship, time, and resources, I realized that a dream can be a flight of fancy. It can be helpful, even exciting, but not necessarily God's plan for you. We each have a dream, but sometimes those original dreams fade and are replaced. That's where God steps in and builds us back up and gives us a new dream. When we back that dream up with a solid vision, strategy, brand, communication, prayer, and action, we can win!"

I have learned through tragedy, prayer, and great mentorship that a vision for your life can be revealed to you and can still come true. Did I mention great mentorship?

He smiled again at the crowd as he thought of JJ and looked at his parents, Bambi, Kelly, Ranger, and his wife. The audience could sense love and appreciation in Elliott's heart for all who helped him get to where he is today. They were fully engaged now and hanging on to every word he was saying.

I learned, and it was a bit of a surprise to me, that hockey wasn't the key to my purpose in life. You see our purpose cannot depend on athletic performance, which is such a temporary and unpredictable platform. I learned that when a vision has strategy, when a vision has a brand, when a vision has a good communication plan, that is covered in prayer, then and only then, can we properly act. Taking an action is the last step of this process because we need time to work through all the steps, in order for the vision to succeed. This is a plan and process to win. Vision only wins when we work the vision! And working the vision through strategy, brand, communication, prayer, and action is a tested process that works. Are you picking up what I am putting down?

Elliott paused. Looking out at the crowd, he could tell they were with him. Most were staring right at him, but others were taking notes, or scrambling to catch up with him. He took a deep breath and said, *who likes to lose? Raise your hand if you like to lose.* No one raised their hand.

He continued, *Ok, ok, ok, so raise your hand if you like to win.*

Nearly every hand was raised.

Maybe you were taking notes or were a little distracted. He lowered his voice. Raise your hand if you like to win.

More hands went up. He slightly raised his voice. *Raise your hand if you like to win?* He raised his voice even louder and said, *raise your hand if you like to win!*

Now, everyone in the crowd had their hand up. Elliott was so nervous about this part. He had the crowd pumped and ready to win. There was not one person in that room who didn't have their hand up. Some people were so into it they stood up and were jumping with both hands in the air.

"Ok awesome," he said. But he was thinking OMG they have bought in. He knew he had to be confident for this next part. *OK, what does it mean for everyone here? This means that we are going to win. I sit here before you with a vision that is short, portable, easy to understand, memorable, inspiring and has the God factor. I am so fired up to share with you a plan to win.*

My mentors over the years have shown me that someone without a plan, is someone who is planning to lose. Today there are no losers in this crowd. Today we are going to win, and we are going to win big!

THE SPEECH

Today, I am here soliciting your advice, time, and resources. Today, I am here to start the process to end Modern-Day Slavery in the world and I need your help.

My vision that God helped me to discover is to End Modern-Day Slavery!

Everyone in the crowd shuffled in their seat, as if they could not find a more comfortable position. Some stood up and clapped with excitement.

"We are going to end Modern-Day Slavery! I'll say it again. We are going to end Modern-Day Slavery!"

The crowd clapped and went wild starting to chant, "Win, win, win, win!"

Today is the UN International Day for the abolition of slavery, which signifies that the General Assembly of the United Nations will adopt a vision for the suppression of human trafficking and exploitation. I am here today to inspire and empower you with a God-given vision to end Modern-Day Slavery! Today we win!

Our Strategy to execute this vision is to raise awareness of this global tragedy and focus on the eradication of all contemporary forms of slavery. These forms include human trafficking, sexual exploitation, the worst forms of child labor, forced marriage, and the forced recruitment of children for use in armed conflict. We are going to raise awareness by getting people involved with their time, resources, and money. It's an unfair fight and our strategy will engage hundreds of millions of people with their voices, time, and resources because you are all winners and want to win, in this global epidemic. We will create awareness and destroy this ruthless, godless, ecosystem of losers.

As you already know, Elliott said to the now highly motivated group of influencers, *most child labor that occurs today is for economic exploitation. Contrary to the convention on the rights of the child, which recognizes 'the right of the child to be protected from economic exploitation and from performing any work that is likely to be hazardous or to interfere with the child's education, or to be harmful to the child's health or physical, mental, spiritual, moral or social development.' With this new vision and strategy, we will change the brand and the brand promise over the next three to five years by promising to expose these wrong doings and create awareness of this morally corrupt industry. We will communicate this new brand message and our vision to every corner of the earth. We will have prayer teams all over the world, praying for families and children of child labor and slave labor. As we sit here today, we are taking action through these steps."*

As Elliott said "steps," the actual R7 steps flashed up on the screen all around the room and everyone's eyes pivoted from Elliott to the PowerPoint presentation. It was a plain slide that had these words on it

THE SPEECH

Step 1: Destiny–Glorify Him

Step 2: Vision–End Modern-Day Slavery

Step 3: Strategy–Create Awareness, ask for time, resources, advice and money

Step 4: Brand–Build 'End Slavery brand' through all touchpoints

Step 5: Communicate the 'End Slavery' vision through all touch points

Step 6: Prayer–Constantly pray about steps 1-5, everyday

Step 7: Action–Mobilize End Slavery Vision–Never stop

---

1) Destiny
Glorify Him

2) Vision
End Modern Day Slavery

3) Strategy
Create awareness; ask for time, resources, advice, and money.

4) Brand
Build 'End Slavery' brand through all touchpoints.

5) Communicate
Communicate the 'End Slavery' vision through all touchpoints.

6) Prayer
Constantly pray about steps 1 - 5, every day.

7) Action
Mobilize 'End Slavery' vision - never stop.

VISION WINS

Elliott looked up at the PowerPoint and said, *Ladies and gentlemen, as I am winding down this message, I want to tell you that I didn't come here to give you a speech. I came here to empower you and welcome you to a new era. A new vision has emerged, a vision that will change the future of Modern-Day Slavery. I am here today to communicate that vision to you. What we have been doing so far has not been working! Will you join me in the fight against Modern-Day Slavery? Will you become an influencer and support this vision with your voice? Will you support this vision with your resources? Will you support it with your precious time, and money? We need to reset our ideas on Modern-Day Slavery. We need to change our mindset and approach. I believe with all my heart that with mentors and each one of you helping spread the word that we can end Modern-Day Slavery. Will you join me today? I repeat, will you join me today?"*

The crowd started clapping and didn't stop. It went from clapping to a standing ovation, to standing, clapping, and whistling.

As he was getting ready to leave the stage, he closed by saying, *scoring a goal in front of thousands of people and getting drafted in the NHL are all amazing accomplishments. I am forever grateful for those amazing memories. When I reflect on those accomplishments, I see how I felt like I was at the peak of my dream. However, after sharing God's vision and purpose with you here today, I have never felt more empowered, respected, and loved by my*

THE SPEECH

Heavenly Father. I am humbled and grateful for this new life and vision God has given me to walk with Him and to share with you.

Elliott's heart felt warm and fulfilled. He knew this vision, God's vision to set the prisoners free, would impact millions of lives through several generations of men and women who might one day become doctors, lawyers, senators, entrepreneurs, community leaders and coaches.

The applause and cheering continued as he turned and wheeled himself off the stage. Nobody felt bad for him now. No, everybody felt empowered by Elliott's life and vision. They realized he was not limited by his physical abilities. His vision, passion, and purpose to end Modern-Day Slavery gave him unlimited potential. The crowd was empowered by his vision and the R7 steps. In his heart, he sent warm gratitude up to JJ.With a smile on his face, he turned, waved, and left the audience with one final thought....

VISION WINS...ALWAYS!

VISION WORKSHEET

When beginning to write your personal or corporate vision statement there are some guidelines and principles to consider.

Below are key guidelines and principles to consider:

- Review Checklist Vision Checklist

- Answer the question "What is the future I am fighting for?"

- Review other vision statement examples

- Pray about how to whittle your vision statement down to 7 to 11 words

When creating your personal vision, it is important to understand the vision statement checklist

VISION STATEMENT CHECKLIST

Vision Checklist
1) Simple
2) Easy to understand
3) Portable
4) Inspiring
5) Empowering
6) Detailed
7) People Oriented
8) Memorable
9) The God factor (Go outside your personal effort)

VISION WINS

Now that we understand the checklist, let's begin to build the actual sentence. The sentence is 7-11 words with no conjunctions (it is very rare that a conjunction will be used).

The sentence is built on reality and the past, but points to the future. In order for your vision to make an impact it should be shared.

The first question to ask yourself when thinking about your vision is "What is the future I am fighting for?"

Answer this question "What is the future I am fighting for?"

____

____

____

____

____

Here are some great vision statement examples and Vision Architecture examples from executives and athletes that I have the fortunate opportunity to work with over the years.

Steve - Achieving mind blowing dreams for a better world.

Joe - To End Slavery.

Jason - Capturing life moments for every executive and professional athlete on the planet.

VISION WORKSHEET

Susan - Share the life everywhere, every day.

Scott - Transforming lives by building creative outlets everywhere in the world.

Jessica - Capture every heart through creatively communicating the art of being present.

Jesse - Strategically impacting everyone I meet.

Bryce - I impact sports fans daily, everywhere on the planet.

Mark - I maximize everyone's potential for a healthy active life.

Abbi - Transforming the world by healing broken hearts.

Olden – Every day I impact the world for Kingdom purposes.

Mark - I am the best life skills teacher on the planet.

Jon – Every day I am passionate about building hope.

Tayron – Every day I am calm in the storm.

Jessica - Everywhere I go, I help others create order out of chaos.

Krunti - I bring vision to life through sound, everywhere in the world

Donna - I am the greatest helper in the world.

Kid - I discover visual intelligence daily.

Andrew - I am passionate about seeing families succeed, everywhere in the world.

Andrew - I transform lives one person at a time.

VISION WINS

Mark – Every day I create opportunities for elevation.

Neal - I will raise standards all around the world.

Myron - I put God in front of every thought, decision, and victory.

Anna - I create experiences that inspire joy to people of all ages.

Dupsy - Equipping builders in their callings.

John – Every day I build better opportunities.

Hala - I provide supportive environments for building dreams.

Justin J - Impacting the world through creative discovery.

Mike - I am passionate about the pursuit of excellence.

Tanya - I am the voice of hope to the world.

David - To create Christian harmony throughout the world.

Drew - I challenge complacency every single day.

Rick - Everywhere in the world I am inspiring citizens to preserve liberty.

Corey - I inspire and grow others everywhere on the planet.

Ernest - Liberating the world with the love of Christ.

Jeremy - To become a world class athlete.

Sabrina - Every day, I capture moments worth sharing.

Vish - I am a world champion of culture change.

VISION WORKSHEET

Neal - Every minute I love to discover purpose in every situation.

Cathy - I harness the power of theatre for innovation.

Todd - Building a financial empire, every day.

Kelly - Everywhere I walk, I am a catalyst for positive change.

Kofi - I rejuvenate business daily.

Jarret - I inspire creative thought everywhere on the planet.

Patrick - I am radically passionate about the changing generations.

Stephen - To be #1 caring company on the planet.

Gregg - Help people everywhere live the 7 words.

Mark - We maximize everyone's health potential.

Larry - 100 thousand strong.

Hockey Hut - To maximize athletic development, every day.

Seeking Hope - Inspiring hope and healing to everyone in crisis.

FCA Hockey - To impact the world for Jesus, one player at a time.

EXAMPLES OF VISION ARCHITECTURE

THE HOCKEY HUT

Vision: Maximizing athletic development, every day.

Mission Statement(s):

1. We promise to be authentic, honest, and transparent.
2. We promise to be prepared for every session.
3. We promise to deliver a personalized developmental plan.
4. We strive to build trusted, lasting relationships with our athletes and parents.
5. We promise to execute with focused intensity.
6. We promise to be prompt and timely in our communication.

Brand Promise: You will become a better athlete, at every session.

STOA VISION ARCHITECTURE

Vision Statement: Speaking boldly. Changing the world for Christ.

STOA exists within the Christian Homeschool speech and debate community to:

1. Facilitate opportunities for competition and training.
2. Build a world class community.
3. Equip Christian coaches in the art and science of public speaking and debate excellence.
4. Promote the development of a Biblical worldview.
5. Share the benefits of speech and debate around the world.
6. Start new Stoa speech and debate clubs around the world.

Core Values:

1. We are committed to following established policies and procedures.
2. We are organized and communicate effectively.
3. We promote transparency and servant leadership.
4. We communicate a clear vision and mission.
5. We promote integrity and honesty in every situation.
6. We recognize competitive excellence.

Brand Promise: We promote opportunities for Christian homeschool speech and debate.

HORN GOALTENDING
VISION ARCHITECTURE

Vision Statement: Every day I develop athletes to reach their maximum potential.

Mission Statements:

1. We are passionate about promoting athletes.
2. We strive to build Intimate relationships with athletes.
3. We mentor athletes on a daily.
4. We develop goaltenders to reach their full potential.
5. We are passionate about raising future community leaders.

Core Values:

1. We are passionate about building trusted relationships.
2. We are resourceful in every situation.
3. We are thoughtful of everyone's concerns.
4. We are honest in our communication.
5. We love spending time with family.

Brand Promise: We create an environment for athletic growth and development.

HOPE REINS VISION ARCHITECTURE

Vision Statement: We Inspire true hope and healing for every child.

Mission Statements:

1. We comfort the hurting and broken with God's redemptive love.
2. We connect hurting children with rescued horses.
3. We offer hope and healing through Jesus Christ
4. We share authentic and transparent stories.
5. We collaborate with organizations that support hurting families.

Core Values:

1. We believe that God is our source, Jesus is the way and the word never changes.
2. We desire honest communication.
3. We are responsible for our actions and words in all situations.
4. We unconditionally love children.
5. We appreciate and love every story.
6. We love authentic and transparent relationships.
7. We seek the lord and treat people with grace in each situation

Hope Reins Brand Promise: We provide opportunities for hope and healing.

SEEKING HOPE VISION ARCHITECTURE

Vision Statement: Inspiring hope to everyone in crisis.

Mission Statements:

1. We provide an emotional support plan through training and development.
2. We reduce stress in the midst of a crisis.
3. We bring the armor of God with Biblical truth to battlefields across America.
4. We inspire organizations to build teams to care for those in crisis.

Core Values:

1. We love people who are transparent and real.
2. We are on time every time.
3. We love and respect people who are passionate about personal development.
4. We love people who are willing to move forward.

Brand Promise: We teach and train emotional first aid techniques rooted in God's promise for hope and change for those in crisis.

ROSALIND MUSIC VISION ARCHITECTURE

Vision: We are connecting isolated people with Jesus through music, every day.

Mission Statements:

1. Finding outreach opportunities to reach the isolated.
2. Connecting the isolated to a Christian church body.
3. Teaching about having a personal relationship with the one true God.
4. Building fully devoted followers of Jesus Christ by offering to speak, sing, or meet and greet church bodies to talk about my testimony for free.

Core Values:

1. I value the ability to follow God given rights.
2. I value and appreciate restraint and self-discipline.
3. I value self-awareness and self-reflection.
4. I appreciate God directed human morality.

THIS SEASON'S COLORS
VISION ARCHITECTURE

Vision: Bringing unity to every community.

Mission:

We aspire to bring unity to our community through:

1. Encouraging
2. Connecting
3. Advocating
4. Empowering
5. Giving

Core Values:

1. We appreciate good listeners.
2. We love communities and families that are in unity with each other and their heavenly father.
3. We value quality customer service.
4. We appreciate people who honor their commitments.
5. We love when people use honor the gifts and power they have been given.
6. We appreciate and value people who honor authority.
7. We value the unseen and isolated.

3G (GOD, GROWTH AND GUTS) VISION ARCHITECTURE

Vision: Empowering global movements, every day.

Mission:

1. We want to share Him with the world through God, Growth, and Guts.
2. We want to encourage, inspire and empower individuals.
3. We will share Him with the world through God by preaching and speaking and providing encouragement.
4. We will share Him with the world through growth by providing discipleship, mentorship, emotional, and academic inspiration.
5. We will share Him with the world with relevancy and guts by empowering individuals with the plan, evangelism, faith, and confidence to move forward on their God given dreams and aspirations.

Core Values:

1. We appreciate people who are empowered by their power and authority.
2. We love empowered individuals.
3. We love to empower individuals and teams.
4. We love people who seek and fight for their self-worth.
5. We love to inspire groups of people.

Build Brand Promise: We open the door for inspiration and empowerment.